Advance Acclaim for *Monochrome Days*

"No one can understand the mind of a young adult better than a young adult herself. In *Monochrome Days*, Irwin uses personal experience and professional insight to arm teens with the tools they need to conquer the beast of depression. The book includes information about the thoughts and feelings teens are experiencing or see their friends experiencing, with suggestions as to how to talk to parents and other trusted loved ones. By conveying this information by telling her own story, Irwin arms young adults with the most important knowledge of all: that through it all, they are not alone.

"With so many teens facing challenges to their mental health every day, this book is a must-read for all teenagers and the adults that love them."

—Alison Malmon, Founder and
Executive Director, Active Minds, Inc.

"An honest, helpful, and hopeful account of one teen's journey from pain to promise. *Monochrome Days* takes the mystery out of depression and provides real guidance to teens who may struggle with this illness, as well as to their friends and families."

—Jerry Reed, M.S.W., Executive Director,
Suicide Prevention Action Network USA

"This book is of great value to people of all ages—however, particularly to adolescents. Cait skillfully manages to make 'fear of the unknown'—so often experienced by teens when diagnosed with depression and other mental illnesses—a non-issue. This book leaves no stone unturned. While sharing her story, Cait quite effectively combats the stigma and misconceptions so often associated with mental illnesses, especially for teens. She shows that depression is a real illness with mental, emotional, and physical implications and conveys the enormous importance of early diagnosis and treatment."

—Darcy Gruttadaro, J.D., Director,
NAMI Child & Adolescent Action Center

"Sometimes, only those who have been in dark places can provide the light for others to get out. Cait Irwin provides a wonderfully clear-eyed and brave look at depression in teenagers, which is so often undiagnosed or shrugged off as 'moodiness.' Without melodrama or self-pity, she takes us through the whole experience, and shows how medication, therapy, love, and the creative spark can combine to heal a ravaged mind."

—Tracy Thompson, author of
The Beast: A Journey Through Depression

JB

The Annenberg Foundation Trust at Sunnylands'
Adolescent Mental Health Initiative

Patrick E. Jamieson, Ph.D., *Series Editor*

In addition to *Monochrome Days,* other books in this series for young people are planned on the following topics:

Addiction (2007)
Eating Disorders (2007)
Obsessive-Compulsive Disorder (2007)
Schizophrenia (2007)
Social Anxiety Disorder (2007)
Suicide Prevention (2007)

Available now:

Mind Race: A Firsthand Account of One Teenager's Experience with Bipolar Disorder (2006)
Patrick E. Jamieson, Ph.D., with Moira A. Rynn, M.D.

Also available in the series for parents and other adults:

If Your Adolescent Has Depression or Bipolar Disorder (2005)
Dwight L. Evans, M.D., and Linda Wasmer Andrews

If Your Adolescent Has an Eating Disorder (2005)
B. Timothy Walsh, M.D., and V. L. Cameron

If Your Adolescent Has an Anxiety Disorder (2006)
Edna B. Foa, Ph.D., and Linda Wasmer Andrews

If Your Adolescent Has Schizophrenia (2006)
Raquel E. Gur, M.D., Ph.D., and Ann Braden Johnson, Ph.D.

Monochrome Days

A Firsthand Account of One Teenager's Experience with Depression

Cait Irwin

with Dwight L. Evans, M.D., and Linda Wasmer Andrews

The Annenberg Foundation Trust at Sunnylands'
Adolescent Mental Health Initiative

2007

OXFORD
UNIVERSITY PRESS

Oxford University Press, Inc., publishes works that
further Oxford University's objective of excellence
in research, scholarship, and education.

The Annenberg Foundation Trust at Sunnylands
The Annenberg Public Policy Center of the University of Pennsylvania
Oxford University Press

Oxford New York
Auckland Cape Town Dar es Salaam Hong Kong Karachi
Kuala Lumpur Madrid Melbourne Mexico City Nairobi
New Delhi Shanghai Taipei Toronto

With offices in
Argentina Austria Brazil Chile Czech Republic France Greece
Guatemala Hungary Italy Japan Poland Portugal Singapore
South Korea Switzerland Thailand Turkey Ukraine Vietnam

Published by Oxford University Press, Inc.
198 Madison Avenue, New York, NY 10016
www.oup.com

Library of Congress Cataloging-in-Publication Data

Irwin, Cait.
Monochrome days : a firsthand account of one teenager's experience
with depression / by Cait Irwin with Dwight L. Evans and Linda Wasmer Andrews.
p. cm. — (Adolescent mental health initiative)
Includes bibliographical references and index.

ISBN 978-0-19-531005-4 (pbk)
1. Irwin, Cait—Mental health.
2. Depressed persons—United States—Biography—Juvenile literature.
3. Depression in adolescence—United States—Juvenile literature.
I. Evans, Dwight L.
II. Andrews, Linda Wasmer.
III. Title.
RJ506.D4I79 2007 616.85'270092—dc22 [B] 2006023381

9 8 7 6 5 4
Printed in the United States of America
on acid-free paper

Contents

Foreword

The Adolescent Mental Health Initiative (AMHI) was created by The Annenberg Foundation Trust at Sunnylands to share with mental health professionals, parents, and adolescents the advances in treatment and prevention now available to adolescents with mental health disorders. The Initiative was made possible by the generosity and vision of Ambassadors Walter and Leonore Annenberg, and the project was administered through the Annenberg Public Policy Center of the University of Pennsylvania in partnership with Oxford University Press.

The Initiative began in 2003 with the convening, in Philadelphia and New York, of seven scholarly commissions made up of over 150 leading psychiatrists and psychologists from around the country. Chaired by Drs. Edna B. Foa, Dwight L. Evans, B. Timothy Walsh, Martin E.P. Seligman, Raquel E. Gur, Charles P. O'Brien, and Herbert Hendin, these commissions were tasked with assessing the state of scientific research on the prevalent mental disorders whose onset occurs predominantly between the ages of 10 and 22. Their collective findings now appear in a book for mental health professionals and policymakers titled *Treating and Preventing Adolescent Mental Health Disorders* (2005). As the first product of the Initiative, that book also identified a research agenda that would best advance our ability to prevent and treat these disorders, among them anxiety disorders, depression and bipolar disorder, eating disorders, substance abuse, and schizophrenia.

The second prong of the Initiative's three-part effort is a series of smaller books for general readers. Some of the books are designed primarily for parents of adolescents with a specific mental health disorder. And some, including this one, are aimed at adolescents themselves who are struggling with a mental illness. All of the books draw their scientific information in part from the AMHI professional volume, presenting it in a manner that is accessible to general readers of different ages. The "teen books" also feature the real-life story of one young person who has struggled with—and now manages—a given mental illness. They serve both as a source of solid research about the illness and as a roadmap to recovery for afflicted young people. Thus they offer a unique combination of medical science and firsthand practical wisdom in an effort to inspire adolescents to take an active role in their own recovery.

The third part of the Sunnylands Adolescent Mental Health Initiative consists of two websites. The first, www.CopeCareDeal.org, addresses teens. The second, www.oup.com/us/teenmentalhealth, provides updates to the medical community on matters discussed in *Treating and Preventing Adolescent Mental Health Disorders*, the AMHI professional book.

We hope that you find this volume, as one of the fruits of the Initiative, to be helpful and enlightening.

Patrick Jamieson, Ph.D., *Series Editor*
Adolescent Risk Communication Institute
Annenberg Public Policy Center
University of Pennsylvania
Philadelphia, PA

Preface

Society tends to shrug off depression as just a minor annoyance or passing phase, especially when the person who has it happens to be a teenager or young adult. But if you've ever felt it, you know that's a lie. Full-blown depression is an excruciating disease. It drains your hope, saps your energy, and steals all the fun from your life.

This is a painfully honest account of my own struggle with major depression, which began when I was 14. When my depression first struck, I had no idea what it was or how to fight back. All I knew was that I suddenly felt hopeless, helpless, and completely alone. In the 11 years since then, I've put a name to the overwhelming sense of emptiness and despair. I've learned that depression is a real and serious disease—just as real as asthma and diabetes. And I've found that, like many other diseases, this one is treatable. With medication and psychotherapy—plus a healthy dose of self-help—I ultimately managed to take back my life and rediscover my reasons for living it.

What's in This Book for You

If you are a high school student or young adult waging your own struggle against depression—or if you care about someone else who is—this book is for you. It's the book I wish someone had handed me more than a decade ago. I'm not here to preach or judge. I'm simply here to let you know that you are *not* alone, no matter how isolated you might feel. It's estimated that 4% of adolescents become seriously depressed each year. My first-hand experience of depression may be different from yours in some ways, but I think you'll recognize similarities, too.

I have a second goal as well, and that's to share vital information. When depression first entered my life, I didn't know what was wrong or where to turn for help. I had to figure things out the hard way, but I want it to be easier for you. Think of this book as your cheat sheet on depression. In each chapter, I start out by talking about my personal experiences. Then I give you the down-to-earth, up-to-date facts you need to make your own decisions about coping with depression.

I'm an artist, not a psychiatrist. To ensure that the medical and scientific parts of the book are accurate, I have been lucky enough to team up with one of the nation's foremost psychiatric experts on depression. Dr. Dwight L. Evans is a professor of psychiatry, medicine, and neuroscience as well as chairman of the psychiatry department at the University of Pennsylvania School of Medicine. He also is president of the American Foundation for Suicide Prevention. In 2003, Dr. Evans chaired a distinguished professional commission on adolescent mood disorders. This commission was convened by the Annenberg Foundation Trust at Sunnylands, a nonprofit group that aims to enhance mental health among young people. Much of the scientific information in this book comes from a report issued by the Annenberg commission. By combining my personal experiences with Dr. Evans's professional expertise, this book helps you look at depression from every angle.

The third person on our writing team is Linda Wasmer Andrews, a journalist who has specialized in mental health issues for more than two decades. One of the ways she contributed was by interviewing several young men with depression who were kind enough to give us the guy's-eye view of this illness. You'll find their stories in sidebars sprinkled throughout the book. All the stories are true, as are all the events I've recounted from my own life. However, we've used fictitious names in the sidebars and at some points in my story to protect people's privacy.

Together, my coauthors and I have created a book that specifically addresses the concerns of adolescents of both sexes—concerns that I discovered are often ignored elsewhere. Depression is a complex problem, and this book doesn't offer easy solutions. But it does provide a starting point for taking action and getting help.

Why I'm Revisiting the Beast

I'll admit it: Writing about the worst time of my life hasn't been a picnic. There are details I would rather leave buried deep in one of those dark places where unwelcome memories hide. While writing this book, I have been reliving experiences that were utterly miserable and deeply distressing the first time around. By now, you're probably asking the obvious question: If these memories are so unpleasant, why write about them?

For me, sharing my struggles is a way of releasing them. In fact, if there is one thing I have learned from depression, it's the value of communicating. Along with writing, I naturally tend to communicate through art. I began keeping a sketchbook journal about depression in high school. It eventually grew into my first published book, *Conquering the Beast Within.* After high school, I studied studio art in college and later established my own art-for-hire business in northern Wisconsin, through which I've received commissions for everything from murals to wood carvings. Although I've tackled a wide range of subjects in my art, I think much of my best work draws from the same deep well of emotion that was the source of so much pain during my depression.

I also have become an outspoken advocate for mental health as well as an official spokesperson for the Suicide Prevention Action Network USA. I find it empowering to express myself through words and images, to unearth what is buried deep inside. If I can help others in the process, that's a wonderful bonus. And if I can help break down the stigma that is still attached to mental illness, that's another powerful reason to open up.

My ultimate hope is that you may see yourself in my story and realize that you, too, can overcome this invisible illness. Depression can feel unchangeable, but that's a nasty trick the disease plays on your mind. In truth, it is something you *can* change with effort, patience, and the help of appropriate treatment. If you are looking for the inspiration and information to get started, you've come to the right place.

Monochrome Days

Chapter One

The Clouds Roll In: Introduction to Depression

My Story

The beeping of the alarm clock sounded distant in my half-awake dream. As I opened my eyes, the muted beep seemed to amplify into a loud blast. My body was jolted awake, but my mind was still reluctant. I was hesitant to acknowledge the beginning of another day that was sure to be just as dreary as the one before and the one to follow.

Grudgingly, I swung my legs out of bed. Then I sat there in the cold February morning while I waited for my mind to catch up to my body. I began to think about the odd feeling that had been quietly creeping around inside my mind for the past month or so. I couldn't quite pinpoint this feeling—what caused it, why it had suddenly appeared out of nowhere. Was it really growing day by day, or was I just imagining that?

A dark, brooding cloud was slowly casting a shadow across my mind. While I had never been an early riser, this felt different from simply being tired after staying up too late the night before. I felt weighed down, oppressed by the burden of having to face a new day. I was just waking up, and I was already exhausted by the idea of what lay ahead. The mind-cloud was starting to cast my reality in a different light.

My Life Before the Clouds

It wasn't always this way. Depression came into my life around the middle of eighth grade. Before that, I had been the kind of friendly little kid who would stare at strangers until they finally gave up and smiled back. I liked to play and laugh and sing silly made-up songs. I did have a sensitive side—some might even say oversensitive. I would come home from kindergarten and say things like, "My heart was crushed today because so-and-so got teased." Later, I wondered whether this hypersensitivity had made me more vulnerable to depression. Back then, though, the world still seemed full of light most of the time.

I grew up in a close family, with a mom, dad, older brother, and two bassett hounds named Ward and June Cleaver. My memories from early childhood are mostly happy ones. By the time I was eight, however, the atmosphere in my family had started to change. I no longer spent much time with my dad. He worked the night shift, and even when he was around, he was usually in a bad mood. Looking back, I realize that he had begun to experience his own problems with depression. But at the time, I was simply hurt and confused.

It didn't take long before I gained a reputation at my new school for being a little bit different.

When I was in third grade, my mom loaded up me, my brother, and our new dog and cat (the Cleavers had since passed away), and we moved to my parents' Midwestern hometown. My dad followed a few months later after our old house sold. It didn't take long before I gained a reputation at my new school for being a little bit different. I think it was the short animated film I brought for show and tell that sealed it. I had created the film with the help of my dad and an eight-millimeter camera. It starred five animated drops of water who played Guns N' Roses' "Welcome to the Jungle" in a rock band. The reputation I got that day—creative, but different—stayed with me throughout my school years.

By sixth grade, it had become painfully clear to me that not everyone appreciates those who march to their own beat. My teacher that year made it her mission to break down my spirit. She was determined that I had to "live in the real world" and "stop using creativity as a crutch." She started small, by calling on me when I obviously didn't know the answer. But before I knew it, I was knee-deep in homework corrections and detentions. With nothing to lose, I began to argue back. Eventually, the confrontations grew so heated and frequent that I wound up being transferred to another sixth-grade class.

I had learned a valuable lesson, although I doubt it's the one my teacher had in mind. I realized that there were basically two roads I could choose: Either I could be who I was or I could blend in with the crowd. For me, it was an easy choice to stay true to myself. When I started junior high the next year, I quickly carved out my niche as class clown and resident artist. I enjoyed hanging out with friends, working on art projects, and walking in the woods. But at times, it felt as if all my classmates were changing into each other, and there wasn't much room for someone who was one of a kind.

What's Wrong With Me?

I had survived these little tests of spirit. Still, nothing had prepared me for the heavy clouds of depression that rolled into my life midway through eighth grade. One particular morning as I sat on the edge of my bed, I felt a crushing sense of hopelessness that was unlike anything I had ever experienced before. I

I was bogged down in the inertia of despair.

knew that I needed to get moving if I wanted to avoid being late for school, but I was bogged down in the inertia of despair.

"Hurry up! The weight room is only open for an hour." I was yanked from my thoughts by my brother, Andy, yelling impatiently. Without thinking, I threw on some clothes and hurried down the stairs. My parents had long since started their workdays, and it was my brother's job to take me to school now that he had his school driving permit. By the time I made it outside, Andy had already been sitting in his '65 Willis Jeep truck a few minutes too long. I threw my backpack into the truck bed and climbed in. "The defrost isn't working, so try not to breathe too much," he said in that loving brotherly way.

Riding to school in his old rickety truck with rusty struts, I looked at my brother with true, but well-hidden, admiration. I know it's common for even close siblings to grow more distant during their teen years. But the two-year difference in our ages was only a small part of what was pushing us apart. We were polar opposites in nearly every way. I suspected that I was an embarrassment for my brother because I was not just a bratty little sister, but a bratty little sister who was on the eccentric side. That morning, my suspicions were confirmed when Andy looked down at my shoes, rolled his eyes, and asked why I needed to wear them.

Glancing at my feet, I could almost understand his animosity. Yes, the shoes were over the top. Technically, they met the school dress code requiring hard-soled shoes that laced up the front. My hard-soled shoes just happened to be old patent leather men's formal footwear, doctored up with leopard print plush and a ton of superglue. My brother didn't understand my reasoning, but I knew that I needed to spice up the dress code. It was how I expressed myself.

The rest of our short ride to school was spent in silence. My brother was already navigating the day to come in his brain, I thought. He had his goals in mind, he always did what he needed to do, and he did it efficiently. I was envious of the way he seemed to have things under control. I thought there was no possible way he would ever let a dark cloud settle upon *his* brain. When we arrived at school, Andy jumped out of the truck and made a beeline for the weight room.

I had almost an hour to kill before my first class. I took my time about going into the school building, despite the freezing weather. Mentally, I was able to delay the start of the school day as long as I didn't go through that door. Out in the student parking lot, it hit me that I had never felt this way before. Lately, all it took was a tiny setback, and I would find myself choking down a gush of tears. It had happened just the afternoon before at basketball practice, when I spaced out during a line drill and the coach hollered at me. Since when did the slightest of glitches have the power to affect me this way? *What's wrong with me?* I wondered.

> All it took was a tiny setback, and I would find myself choking down a gush of tears.

The Darkness Deepens

As the weeks went by, it became harder and harder to wake up in the morning. My mind felt cloudier with each passing day, but my body continued to go robotically through the motions of being a junior high student. Whenever I could, I sought out sanctuary in the school art room. I felt safe there. I was working on a large pen-and-ink poster. It wasn't complicated, and it had no particularly profound meaning, but working on it was my greatest source of comfort.

Outside the art room was a very different story. I felt lost in the press of students walking through the hall on their way to class. I jumped every time someone shouted over my shoulder, and my skin crawled at the sound of all those doors opening and shutting. Once I made it to my classroom, I usually relaxed a little. But that's when my mind would wander back to the cloud.

I recall a typical day sitting in earth science class. I didn't bring my sketchpad; I didn't feel like getting into any trouble. I just wanted to make it through class as uneventfully as possible. In my head, I counted down the minutes. My textbook was open, but I wasn't reading it or listening to the lecture. I was looking at my classmates, wishing I could peer inside their minds. Did they ever feel this way, or was I the only one?

I was sliding downhill fast, and I didn't know what had pushed me over the edge or how to stop the descent. All I knew was that I couldn't pay attention to the science lecture even if I tried. I was too busy holding back the emotional outburst that always seemed to be lurking in wait. The stress had my stomach constantly tied up in knots. My teachers weren't concerned, though. I was 14, and moodiness was to be expected at that age. For a while, I found reassurance in this idea. It meant that there would soon be an end in sight.

But as the weeks passed, it became harder to believe this comforting fiction. My friends might have been a little moody, but they still thought life was worth the effort of living. Something else had seized control of my mind. I was always so tired, but sleep was hard to come by. My appetite was waning, my vision seemed to be growing worse, and my brain felt unable to absorb new information. Meanwhile, my hearing seemed to be growing super-sensitive, to the point where the sounds of a typical school day were often an agony to endure. Somehow, I didn't think these changes were a normal part of puberty.

The darkness was spreading inside me like a cancer. I was radiating negativity on the outside as well as the inside now. Family and friends had started to notice the change in me. My mom, in particular, saw that school was becoming more and more of a challenge. By the end of the spring semester, my grades had slipped, and I had lost a lot of weight. She tried to be encouraging, saying, "Just make it through the next couple of weeks, and then you can enjoy the summer." But her encouragement, which usually served as a lifeline for me, didn't help this time. I trudged through those final days of eighth grade, with each day seeming harder to get through than the last. My physical symptoms were steadily worsening, and I was too worn down to interact with others. I just wanted to be alone in my misery.

Softball and Hard Truths

Finally, the last day of school arrived. The summer vibe was all around, and the halls were chaotic with students hastily cleaning out their lockers. The garbage bins that dotted the halls were overflowing with old tests, term papers, and bag lunches. Out with the old, in with whatever new experiences lay ahead. I was just removing the last of the trash wedged into the bottom of my locker when a group of friends stopped by to ask about my softball plans. Since we had now officially finished eighth grade, we could try out for the junior varsity team. I had been playing sports with most of these girls since third grade, so I didn't want to let them down. More importantly, I didn't want to let *myself* down. I didn't want to give the beast that had invaded my body the satisfaction of keeping me from a game I loved. Since I wouldn't be dealing with school over the summer, I thought I could muster up the energy to play ball.

I decided to try out. My mom was relieved that I was showing an interest in something, and I was determined not to miss a season. I had seen what happened to other athletes who got sick or hurt and were out for a while. Returning to a sport after a long absence looked difficult and frustrating, and I didn't want to blow my chance to move up on the team as I got older.

In the locker room getting ready for tryouts, my best friend, Liz, was excited about my decision to play. I could see in her face how happy she was that we would be spending more time together. We used to take turns staying over at each other's houses, but lately I didn't have the energy to spend much time away from home. I knew she was worried about me.

After we were dressed, Liz and I made our way to the softball field with a small group of classmates. No one talked on the walk over. All I could hear were the sounds of our cleats grinding the gravel road that connected the locker room to the playing field. We were nervous, because as prefreshmen, we were on the lowest rung of the athletic ladder. I knew what to expect; I had seen my brother go through it. We would get ragged on, but I thought I could handle it.

As we approached the field, I heard the coach yell, "All prefresh, get your butts to the equipment shed and grab your gear!" Suddenly, tears filled my eyes and a lump swelled in my throat. I tried desperately to hold back the tears. *I'm so pathetic*, I thought. I wasn't even to the field, and already I wanted to cry. This certainly wasn't the first time I had been yelled at by a coach. It was part of the ritual of playing sports. But on that day, it felt like a personal attack, even though the coach was barking orders to the whole group.

On the way to the equipment shed, I didn't want anyone, even Liz, to see me cry. Liz would ask what was wrong, and I wouldn't be able to answer. The shame of my weakness made me feel hollow. My friends were all laughing and joking around while hauling equipment to the field. I stayed silent, suddenly terrified about how the rest of the day was going to turn out.

Back at the softball field, we barely had time to throw down our gear before we were ordered to get in line and run drills. With the summer sun beating down on us, everyone was sucking in hot air so fast that we looked like fish out of water fighting for a taste of oxygen. After three hours of running, hitting, and fielding drills, we were finally sent home for the night. My friends were all physically exhausted, but I was mentally exhausted as well. It had been tougher than I expected dealing with the harsh comments from upperclassmen and coaches. Every time someone made a remark about my performance, I felt that same lump swell up in my throat again.

The next day was an all-day tryout session. Waking up, I felt as if I had a 20-pound weight attached to each eyelid. Dragging myself out of bed, I briefly thought about eating breakfast, but nothing sounded good. Reluctantly, I gathered my personal gear and headed for the softball field. Taking my usual shortcut through the cemetery, I started second-guessing myself: Could I handle the hazing after all? And could I handle playing if I did make the team?

Once I arrived at the playing field, it was a repeat of the previous day, only more intense. For an hour, the varsity pitcher fired balls across the plate to test our hitting ability. I managed to smash eight of the ten pitches, sending the ball deep into the outfield. The coach seemed pleased, but all I could focus on were the two pitches I had let get past the plate. After a round of heavy fielding drills, we began to jog around the field one more time. I was lagging behind. Speed was never my strong suit, even under the best of circumstances. But somehow it mattered more that day. Nobody was watching, yet I was sure they were all laughing at me.

Just as I finished running, the coach began reading off the names of those who had made the team and the positions they would play. When he called my name and said I would be a junior varsity catcher, I should have been thrilled. I wasn't. In fact, I had secretly hoped that I wouldn't make the team. A whole season of softball loomed in front of me like a mountain that I was feeling much too tired to climb.

No More Sunny Days

The next two weeks of practices dragged on like an eternity. Finally, it was time for my parents, brother, and me to leave on vacation. We were headed to a family reunion, which was being held at a relative's summer home in Florida. I had been looking forward to this trip for months.

Everyone was so glad to see each other after years of being apart, and the house was soon full of laughter and storytelling. That first night, after enjoying some peel-and-eat shrimp, a group of us walked down to the beach to catch the sunset. The sky had already turned a brilliant shade of orange. The air was warm and salty, and the soft, white sand squished under my bare feet.

Suddenly, a dark thought broke through my contentment: *You shouldn't enjoy this, because soon you'll have to leave and return to your normal, sad existence.* I immediately recognized the source of that thought. It was the beast, the dark force that had seized control of my life. This time, though, the beast seemed to have gained power. At that moment, I understood that it didn't matter where I was and what I was doing, because I would always carry the beast inside me.

It was the beast, the dark force that had seized control of my life.

After returning from the beach, my parents and I retired to an apartment above the garage, where we were staying. I stretched out on the couch, and my mom sat down next to me. "This is your vacation," she reassured me. "Try not to think about your problems. Just let your battery recharge." She obviously could see that I still had worries on my mind. After she said goodnight, I tried to fall asleep, but I was tossing and turning. The brief spark of happiness that I had felt on the beach had died away. The clouds were following me everywhere now.

The Big Picture

Looking back, I'm sometimes tempted to wonder why it took so long for us to recognize the cloud for what it was. But then I remember how little we all knew about depression at the time. Like most people, I occasionally dropped the word "depressed" into casual conversation to describe someone who was down in the dumps or feeling a little blue. As I found out later, though, doctors and therapists mean something a bit different when they use the term "depression."

In medical terms, pervasive and long-lasting problems such as the ones I was having are referred to as *major depression.* Throughout the rest of this book, when I talk about depression, I'll primarily have major depression in mind. This is a mental disorder that involves being either sad or irritable nearly all the time, or losing interest or enjoyment in almost everything. These feelings last for at least two weeks, and they cause significant distress or difficulty with everyday tasks. The feelings also occur along with other symptoms, such as:

When I talk about depression, I'll primarily have major depression in mind.

- Excessive weight gain or weight loss without trying
- Increase or decrease in appetite
- Trouble falling or staying asleep, or sleeping too much
- Movements that seem overly keyed up or unnaturally slowed down
- Constant tiredness or lack of energy
- Feelings of worthlessness or inappropriate guilt
- Reduced ability to concentrate, think clearly, or make decisions
- Repeated thoughts of death or suicide

I'll explain more about these symptoms in Chapter 2. But just by glancing at the list, you can see that depression does much more than make you feel sad. It's a disease that affects your whole being—mentally, emotionally, and physically.

Alone in an Unhappy Crowd

When I was suffering from depression, I often felt alone, even when I was surrounded by a caring family and concerned friends. I couldn't imagine that anyone else had ever felt the way I was feeling. There was a grain of truth in that. No two people experience depression in exactly the same way. Nevertheless, depression is a common problem—much more common than many people realize.

No two people experience depression in exactly the same way.

It's hard to say precisely how many teenagers and young adults have depression. In studies looking at this question, researchers have measured depression by a variety of methods, which makes it tricky to compare numbers from one study to the next. However, some of the best figures to date come from the National Comorbidity Survey (NCS). This survey conducted in the early 1990s included more

Other Forms of Depression

Besides major depression, there are two other common types of depressive disorders:

- *Dysthymia* produces symptoms that are similar to major depression, although less severe. But while the symptoms are milder, they can still cause considerable suffering, because they hang around for a year or more. It's similar to the difference between chronic, mild allergies and a bad case of flu. The flu hits you harder, but in the long run, both diseases can have a serious impact on the quality of your life.
- *Bipolar disorder*—also called manic depression—leads to severe, cyclic changes in mood. Periods of an overly high mood, called mania, alternate with periods of depression. Sometimes the shifts in mood are rapid and dramatic, but often they are more gradual. During the depressed phase, a person has the same types of symptoms seen in other depressive disorders. During the manic phase, the person has symptoms such as an exaggerated sense of self-importance, racing thoughts, decreased need for sleep, increased talkativeness or activity, wildly risky behavior, and even psychosis. In young people, mania also can take the form of extreme irritability.

than 8,000 Americans from ages 15 to 54. The NCS found that 14% of teens had experienced major depression by age 18. That's one out of every seven teenagers. In the same survey, another 11% of teens had experienced minor depression—a term that's sometimes used when people have a few mild symptoms of depression, but not enough to qualify as major depression. Add this number to the 14% who developed full-blown major depression, and you'll see that one-fourth of teens in this survey had experienced at least some depression-like symptoms by age 18.

Due to the way depression was measured in the original NCS, it's possible that those numbers are a little on the high side.

However, more recent studies also have found a high rate of depression in young people. Take, for example, a study published in *Archives of Pediatric and Adolescent Medicine* in 2004. For this study, researchers gave questionnaires to more than 9,800 students in grades six, eight, and ten from schools across the United States. They found that 18% of students reported having some symptoms of depression. In both sexes, the rate of such symptoms rose as the students got older. For boys, the rate almost doubled between sixth and tenth grades. For girls, it nearly tripled.

Between 2001 and 2003, an updated version of the NCS, called the National Comorbidity Survey Replication (NCS-R), was given to more than 9,200 Americans. This time around, the survey included only adults ages 18 and older. The results showed that 15% of young adults from 18 to 29 had experienced major depression at some point in their lives. While the numbers from all these studies differ slightly, the bottom line is the same: Depression is surprisingly common, and it often starts during adolescence and early adulthood. When I first got depressed, I would look around at my classmates and think that none of them could possibly understand my pain. Now I know there was a good chance some of them either already had depression or would develop it within a few years.

Depression is surprisingly common.

The Gender Gap

During childhood, girls and boys seem to have about the same risk of depression. But starting in the teen years, females are two to three times as likely to become depressed as males—a pattern that continues into adulthood. Scientists are still trying to sort out the reasons for this sex difference. Some women seem to be more vulnerable to depression at times when their

> **Off to an Early Start**
>
> Ask a roomful of people to name some chronic, or long-lasting, diseases, and chances are good they'll mention heart disease, diabetes, or arthritis. While all these conditions can occur in young people, they're much more common in middle-aged and older adults. It's not surprising, then, that most of us associate chronic diseases with our parents and grandparents—not with ourselves. Unlike physical diseases, though, mental illnesses tend to start early in life. The latest data show that half of all cases of mental illness begin by age 14, and three-quarters start by age 24. As a result, the National Institute of Mental Health has dubbed mental illnesses "the chronic diseases of the young."

sex hormones are in flux, such as right after giving birth. It's interesting that the gender gap in depression first shows up around puberty, when sex hormone levels are changing.

On the other hand, puberty is also a time of rapid social and personal change. Being a teenager typically means facing many new sources of stress, such as dealing with sexuality, coping with peer pressure, finding an adult identity, and handling conflict with parents. Some stresses—for example, rape, date violence, teen pregnancy, or social stereotypes—may be different for males and females, as a group. These differences could affect depression rates as well.

Where Depression Comes From

When depression first entered my own life, the biggest question I had was *why?* I couldn't understand where this dark cloud had suddenly come from. As I later discovered, there wasn't a simple answer to my question.

> When depression first entered my own life, the biggest question I had was *why?*

Guy's-Eye View

Just because depression is *less* common in males than females after puberty doesn't mean it is *un*common. In fact, it's estimated that depression affects more than six million men in the United States each year. Unfortunately, men and boys in our society often get the message that depression is somehow weak or unmanly. This negative—and completely untrue—stereotype may make it harder for some to admit that they have the disease and seek professional help when they need it.

"As a male, I felt that people thought I should be able to just get on with my life," says Marcus, who first developed major depression as an 18-year-old college student. "You know, 'life isn't meant to be easy' and 'we all have problems to deal with.' Except that I was feeling so low, with such a big black hole consuming me from the inside out, that any attempt to cope seemed pointless."

"My view of life dimmed until I became totally self-obsessed and dark-minded," Marcus continues. "My friends couldn't see any of the old Marcus they grew up with, and I kept my distance so I wouldn't have to talk to them about what I was feeling. Eventually, the isolation got so bad that my life practically came to a grinding halt. I was living like a recluse in my parents' house."

When Marcus finally did reach out for help, his symptoms began to improve. He gradually overcame his depression through a combination of medication, psychotherapy, and a healthier lifestyle. But he had waited until he was 25 years old—that's seven years of unnecessary suffering. If he could go back and redo that decision, Marcus says he would get treatment sooner rather than later.

Depression is a complex disease with multiple causes. Genetics, biology, psychology, and environment are all part of the mix.

Genetics

Depression runs in some families, much like heart disease and diabetes do. Studies show that teenagers who have close relatives with depression are more likely to develop the disease themselves. In fact, the children of depressed parents have a two to four times increased risk of major depression. They are also more likely to develop depression at a young age and experience repeated episodes.

That doesn't mean you're doomed to depression if a close relative has it, however. Some people whose family tree has depression on nearly every branch go through life without ever becoming depressed themselves. On the flip side, some people with no family history of depression go on to develop the disease. Just as with heart disease and diabetes, other factors affect whether or not you actually get sick. At most, you might inherit a predisposition to depression that makes you more a little more vulnerable than average to the stresses and strains of life.

Biology

Whether inherited or not, depression has been linked to changes in brain chemistry. These changes involve neurotransmitters, chemicals that ferry messages between brain cells. Here's how it works: Brain cells are separated by a tiny space, called a synapse. The sending cell releases a neurotransmitter into this space. Then the neurotransmitter crosses the gap and attaches to a receptor molecule on the receiving cell. There's a catch, however. Neurotransmitters come in many different types, each with its own distinctive shape. A particular neurotransmitter can only fit into a correctly shaped receptor, much as a key can only fit into a matching lock.

Once the message has been delivered, something still has to be done with the neurotransmitter, which remains in the synaptic space. A large molecule, called a transporter, is involved in bringing the neurotransmitter home. Then the neurotransmitter is absorbed back into the cell that originally released it, a process called reuptake. It's a remarkably neat and efficient system.

At times, though, the system goes awry. In some cases, the receptors may be either too sensitive or not sensitive enough to a particular neurotransmitter. In other cases, the sending cells may release too little neurotransmitter, or the transporters may bring it back too soon. Such problems can involve various neurotransmitters, but two that seem to be especially important in depression are serotonin and norepinephrine. *Serotonin* plays a role in mood, and it also helps regulate sleep, appetite, and sexual drive. *Norepinephrine* plays a role in the body's response to stress, and it also helps regulate arousal, sleep, and blood pressure.

In numerous studies, depression has been linked to imbalances in these neurotransmitters. You'll be hearing more about neurotransmitters in Chapter 5, which discusses treatment options. Medications to treat depression work by changing the amount or activity of these critical chemicals within the brain. Interesting new research using sophisticated imaging technology shows that psychotherapy also may lead to physical changes in the brain, and these changes may affect neurotransmitter levels as well. Thus, one way or another, treatment for depression seems to work at least partly by correcting imbalances in brain chemicals.

Psychology

Depression is based in physiology, but psychology affects it, too. One psychological factor that may play a role is explanatory style—the way you habitually explain to yourself in your mind why events happen. People with a pessimistic explanatory style take the glass-half-empty view. They tend to believe that bad events are unchangeable and will undermine everything they do. They also tend to blame themselves for bad events, even ones beyond their control. It's easy to see how such a dim view of oneself and the world could trigger or worsen depression in vulnerable people. A popular form of psychotherapy, called cognitive-behavioral therapy, aims to help people change the irrationally negative beliefs that may be contributing to their depression.

The amount of stress in your life and the way you respond to it are also important factors. Scientifically speaking, stress refers to your body's natural response to any perceived threat—real or imagined, physical or psychological. When faced with a threat, an alarm goes off in your brain. This alarm, in turn, sets off a series of physical changes as your body prepares to fight or flee. Your heart races, your blood pressure rises, your breathing gets faster, and your muscles tense. The stress response can be a lifesaver in a true emergency. When it continues for a long time, however, the strain of constantly being on high alert can start to take a toll on your body and mind.

Depression is one possible consequence of long-term stress. Sometimes, an extremely upsetting event—such as the death of a parent, a physical or sexual assault, or severe bullying—will set off an episode of depression. But there's no one type of stressful event that always has this effect. In fact, some people manage to bounce back from terrible problems or losses. Others who do develop depression are unable to trace it to a single major setback. Instead, depression often seems to be related to several smaller problems piled one upon the other.

Depression often seems to be related to several smaller problems piled one upon the other.

Environment

Depression starts inside your own mind and body, but the outside world can affect the illness indirectly. Take your relationship with your parents, for instance. I'm a prime example of the fact

"My best friend died in a car crash last month, and I'm still crying every day. Am I depressed?"

The death of someone you love is an extremely emotional experience. The pain typically fades with time, but it can take weeks or months to feel back to normal. The fact that you are still grieving is not necessarily unhealthy. Different people grieve at different rates and in various ways. Along with sadness, you may feel disbelief, anger, guilt, or despair. You also may have some physical symptoms, such as loss of appetite, upset stomach, trouble sleeping, and lack of energy. Overall, you might be surprised by how intense your reaction is and how long it lasts.

At times, grief may turn from a painful but normal experience into full-blown depression. In such cases, the distressing feelings and symptoms last for at least two months. Certain symptoms are particularly common when depression has followed in the wake of grief. Watch for feelings of worthlessness, slowed-down movements, difficulty doing everyday tasks, persistent guilt, and frequent thoughts of death (other than thinking about the death of your friend).

Whether you are experiencing depression or ordinary grief, it makes sense to talk to someone if you're having trouble coping with your feelings. Seek out a trusted adviser, such as a parent, teacher, school counselor, religious adviser, or youth leader. Some schools may offer trained peer counselors, or you might join a grief support group. If you're still struggling even with this extra support, a mental health professional can help you work through your feelings.

that even a teenager with lots of parental love and support can get depressed. But a very tense or distant relationship with your parents could contribute to depression if you're already prone to the disease. You might find that an increase in arguments and conflict at home is what sets off an episode of depression. Or you might find that harsh criticism or rejection by your parents just magnifies your own feelings of worthlessness or self-blame.

Friends are another major influence. When you're depressed, you may lack the motivation and energy to keep up your old friendships or form new ones. As a result, you might start to feel like a social outcast, which only adds to your emotional burden. Other people with depression become either the targets of bullies or bullies themselves. Either way, they inevitably wind up feeling worse.

Being the victim of physical or sexual abuse increases your risk of depression, as does growing up in dire poverty or having a parent who is an alcoholic or drug addict. These are all extremely stressful situations, and it's easy to imagine how they might take a toll on your emotional well-being. But many people survive such adversity without ever developing depression. And many people who grow up in stable, middle-class homes such as my own do go on to become depressed.

So where did *my* depression come from? Maybe I had a genetic tendency toward the disease, passed down from my dad. Maybe my personality—especially my hypersensitive side—made me prone to stress and depression. And maybe the pressure of trying to fit in at school and live up to my teachers' and coaches' expectations played a role. Ultimately, though, what really mattered to me was not how I got mired in depression, but how I could get unstuck. Freeing myself wouldn't prove to be easy. Things got worse before they got better.

Chapter Two

The Belly of the Beast: Signs and Symptoms

My Story

The summer before ninth grade, I was glad to be leaving junior high life behind, but the new world I was entering seemed frighteningly bleak. The beast, which had been stalking me for weeks, had me firmly in its grip now.

One day, I was taking a nap on the couch, when suddenly I was awakened by the phone ringing. My mom brought me the phone, saying that my friend Liz was on the line. I answered with a faint hello. "Are you still coming to my birthday party?" Liz asked with a hint of hesitation in her voice.

Instantly, I was struck by a sickening wave of dread and anxiety. *I have to go to her slumber party,* I thought. *I'm her best friend.* But I honestly didn't know if I could manage it. At that moment, all I wanted was to stay safely wrapped inside my cocoon, sheltered from the outside world with all its stressful demands. Yet despite my doubts, I heard myself reassuring Liz that I would be there. What kind of best friend would I be if I missed her fourteenth birthday?

Part of me believed that this party would do me good, but another part believed that it didn't matter where I was, because the same dark cloud would follow me anywhere. How much longer could I keep going back and forth this way? I was getting very tired of my mind constantly contradicting itself, and I didn't know how much more of this inner dialogue I could take.

I was getting very tired of my mind constantly contradicting itself . . .

My mom saw how hesitant I felt, so she asked me what I expected to be the most difficult thing about attending the party. "I don't think I can handle all the people who will be there," I answered. "What if they ask me why I haven't been around?" I worried that if someone asked me what was wrong, I might burst into uncontrollable sobbing. I knew that I wouldn't be able to produce a convenient answer, because I didn't understand what was going on myself.

Mom tried to comfort me by pointing out that I didn't need to explain myself. "You should just go for Liz's sake," she said. "It's only one night, and you might wind up having some fun, too." I reluctantly agreed and began packing a bag for the slumber party. Normally, I created handmade gifts for the people closest to me, and I had planned to draw a picture and frame it for Liz's birthday. That seemed like too much effort, though, so I opted for a store-bought present. I was dragging around in slow motion. By the time I finished packing and my mom drove me to Liz's house, I was the last to arrive.

Ultimate Party Pooper

From the moment I got there, it took every last ounce of my dwindling energy just to act "normal." Every time I smiled or laughed, it was fake. I felt like the saddest person in the world, but I tried hard to mask my true feelings, because I didn't want to poison Liz's party with my negativity.

As the night went on, the effort of pretending to be happy began to wear me down. Twelve of us were spending the night in Liz's finished basement, and everyone else was still going strong, feeding off the energy of the party. But I was exhausted, so I made myself a bed in the corner.

The moment I lay down, the time-honored tradition of torturing the first person to go to sleep kicked into action. In the past, I had joined in the teasing, but now I was just wishing for morning to come. The more my friends razzed me, the more effort it took not to lose my temper. I had been getting so angry so quickly these days. My friends' high-pitched voices grated on my nerves. The sound was as sharp as needles piercing my brain.

Finally, the party began to die down. While the last few girls awake whispered and giggled softly, I pretended to be asleep. That's when the tears started to flow. As I wiped them away quietly, I shrank deeper inside my sleeping bag. Paranoid thoughts filled my mind: *Does Liz hate me because of how I'm acting? Does everyone else see how different I am? Are they all talking about me?* At last, I drifted into a shallow, but much appreciated, sleep.

Does everyone else see how different I am? Are they all talking about me?

The next morning, I was the last one to come upstairs for breakfast. I didn't want the food—everything was flavorless and unappetizing lately. I was feeling weak and nauseated, and I wanted nothing more than to make my escape as soon as possible. When I saw my mom's car pull into the driveway, it was a small blessing. I thanked Liz for the party and wished her a happy birthday. I think she knew I wasn't going to be around much that summer. I had become distant and reclusive, not the same Cait she had known for the past four years.

Liz hugged me before I left. She didn't say much, but I could see the concern in her eyes. Liz had watched the life drain out of me over the past couple of months. At the time, though, neither of us grasped the true depths of my depression. We didn't yet realize how far I would plummet or how soon the emotional crash would come.

Something Is Really *Wrong*

Once in my mom's car, I began sobbing violently. I confided between gasps that I was miserable and didn't know why. "I can't take this anymore," I wailed. I cried so hard that my face turned a dark shade of red and my pulse pounded in my temples. Startled by my desperate tone, my mom realized that it was time to seek professional help. Looking back, I was very fortunate to have someone in my life who recognized the seriousness of my worsening condition.

As soon as we got home, my mom began calling around to set up an appointment for me. Through her job, she had access to an employee assistance program (EAP), which provided a number of services to employees and their family members who were having trouble managing their daily life and emotional well-being. Initially, I would meet with a counselor at the EAP, who could then refer me to another mental health professional for treatment if necessary.

The EAP appointment was still a few days away, so my mom did her best to distract me from my misery. We went to the zoo and for walks in the woods—places she hoped would feed my soul and heal my mind. But I was past feeling pleasure. My mind was rapidly crumbling around me, and my body had turned to lead. I was too tired to walk far, and even getting out of bed seemed to take more energy than it was worth. Many of the things I had loved to do just a few short months ago had become distasteful and exhausting. I felt dead inside, and nothing my mom tried could revive me.

Headaches came and went, dulling and spiking in intensity throughout the day. When I cried, which was much of the time, it felt as if the force of my tears put an enormous amount of pressure on the backs of my eyeballs. With each heartbeat, my head would thump in unison.

Often, the headaches were triggered by noise. My auditory sensitivity was turned up all the way to extra-high, and everyday sounds seemed to be painfully amplified. Once when I went to the grocery store, I had to leave abruptly when the harsh sound of the carts being stacked drove me into a meltdown.

Everyday sounds seemed to be painfully amplified.

Since almost any crowded place was noisy, I began feeling panicky whenever I was surrounded by people. I would be in a crowded room or busy store, when suddenly my skin would start to crawl and I would feel blood rushing into my face. My instincts told me to get out of there right away because the walls were closing in. Then I would start gasping for air as if I were suffocating. When I finally got outside, I would recoil at the sound of children yelling or a loud truck passing. Noise was all around in my environment, and as a result, my anxiety level stayed at high alert.

At the same time, it was getting harder and harder to comprehend written words. My vision was blurry, but since it had changed so suddenly and I had never needed glasses before, I believed that this must be another nasty trick that my mind was playing on me. I had trouble not only seeing words on a page, but also understanding what they meant. Even simple words eluded me at times, as my brain seemed to be systematically unlearning how to read.

Talking for My Life

In the days immediately after Liz's party, my thoughts became darker as my body grew weaker. I wasn't especially nervous about seeing the EAP counselor, but I honestly didn't think talk therapy could help me, either. How could anyone possibly *say* anything that would ease this pressing pain coming from within my own head?

On the appointed day, my mom drove me to the counselor's office. She filled out paperwork in the waiting room while I met with the counselor alone. Even though I didn't believe she could help me, I still volunteered my thoughts and feelings freely. I responded to her questions in slurred speech, telling her about the vile cloud that had gradually engulfed my mind and body. Finally, the counselor asked the Big Question: "Are you having any suicidal thoughts?"

I paused for a moment, then answered honestly, "Yes." It was the first time I had verbalized that particular dark thought. I felt some small sense of relief at finally confiding in someone, but along with the relief came a much larger sense of shame. Admitting to my suicidal thoughts felt like a self-betrayal. The shame fit in well with all the other negative thoughts about myself that seemed to have taken up permanent residence in my mind.

When she called my mom into the office, the counselor told her that I needed treatment. She recommended a therapist named Ms. S., and she lined up an appointment for me with this therapist the following day.

That night, I had a terrible nightmare—worse than any I had ever had before.

In the dream, I was at my own funeral. I had committed suicide, and I was lying in a casket at the end of the viewing room at a funeral parlor. Everyone who had ever known and loved me was there, dressed in heavily starched black clothes. One by one, they would come up to my dead body, touch my face, and then begin wailing under the weight of their grief. I hovered invisibly, a ghost visiting my own farewell from this earth. When I awoke with a jolt, I discovered that I had been crying in my sleep.

Lying there in bed, I resolved that I wouldn't kill myself, because I never wanted to cause such intense emotional pain to my loved ones. I cried for a couple of hours, mentally replaying the nightmare over and over. Although I finally fell asleep, I woke up the next morning with the dark aura of the nightmare still fresh in my mind. I didn't want to talk about the dream—it was much too disturbing—so the car ride with my mom to Ms. S.'s office was quiet.

My Introduction to Therapy

Despite my negative frame of mind, I knew that I liked Ms. S. as soon as I met her. The office had a calming air, decorated with artwork from all the places around the world where she had traveled. Ms. S. was an earthy woman who seemed very grounded. She was a good fit for me.

I had decided that I wanted to turn off the suicidal thoughts, but that was easier said than done. Within a few minutes after meeting me, Ms. S. could see that my mind was still under siege. She recommended that I see a psychiatrist as well as continue my visits with her. A psychiatrist could prescribe any medications I might need, while she continued to provide the talk therapy. Ms. S. suggested Dr. M., a highly regarded psychiatrist whose reputation was reflected in his busy schedule. The first open appointment

I had decided that I wanted to turn off the suicidal thoughts.

time was several days away, but I would be at the top of the list in case of any cancellations.

My mom had to trust that this was the right path to take. She had seen how far and how fast my condition had deteriorated in a matter of days, and I think the wait frightened her more than anything. I was hanging over the mouth of the beast, and my fingers were losing their grip one by one. If I let go, I would drop into the beast's belly, and that would be the end of me. My mom saw me slipping, and she knew that the next few days were going to be about survival.

The Big Picture

By this point, I was getting a terrifyingly close-up look at what the symptoms of depression are all about. Depression is considered a mood disorder, and a mood is a pervasive emotion that colors a person's whole view of the world. To me, depression seemed to cover everything with the gray tinge of gloom.

As I discovered, depression can exact a heavy toll. It causes anguish not only for the person with the disease, but also for friends and family who have to watch the suffering of someone they love. Fortunately, most people with depression—even those with severe symptoms—can be helped to feel better with proper treatment. So while it's a serious condition, it's also a highly treatable one.

Most people with depression . . . can be helped to feel better with proper treatment.

Depression doesn't always look the way you might think it would. Sure, many people with depression feel overwhelmingly sad or empty and cry all the time. But some teens who are

Taking the First Step

You've decided that you need help, but you and your family aren't sure where to begin. Here are some possible starting places:

- Employee assistance program—My mom's first step toward finding help for me was to call the EAP provided by her employer. EAP visits are usually free, but the number of visits and types of services available may be limited. An EAP counselor can screen for mental disorders. However, you may be referred elsewhere for the treatment itself.
- Health insurance—Your parents can also call their health insurance plan and ask about coverage for mental health treatment. If the insurance is provided by a parent's employer, the company benefits manager may be able to answer some questions as well. Insurance coverage for mental health services often isn't as extensive as that for medical services, so it's important to be informed.
- Medicaid—If your parents don't have insurance, you might qualify for services through Medicaid or the State Child Health Insurance Program (SCHIP). These are government programs that provide medical and mental health care to those who meet eligibility criteria. The programs vary from state to state. To find out what your state offers, start with GovBenefits.gov (800-333-4636, www.govbenefits.gov) and Insure Kids Now! (877-543-7669, www.insurekidsnow.gov).
- Community mental health centers—These community facilities provide a wide range of mental health services regardless of ability to pay. The fees are determined on a sliding scale based on a family's income and the cost of services.

Whether you have private insurance or Medicaid, your parents might need to get actively involved to obtain all the services you require. Once you're over 18, if you're no longer covered under your parents' insurance, you'll need to be assertive about speaking up for yourself. That means familiarizing yourself with your insurance and learning about your rights as a consumer. If a managed care company denies a claim, ask how you can appeal the decision. If you need help with the appeals process, local mental health organizations can usually point you in the right direction. The unfortunate reality is that getting coverage for mental health treatment is often harder than for other kinds of medical care. But a little extra effort and ingenuity—and a lot of patience—can go a long way toward getting the care you need.

depressed become cranky and short-tempered instead. Others become extremely apathetic, losing interest or enjoyment in almost everything. For me, depression was a hateful mixture of all these forms of misery combined.

Whatever form it takes, the depressed mood must last for at least two weeks to qualify as major depression. It also must be accompanied by other unpleasant mental, physical, and emotional symptoms. It's no surprise, then, that depression causes considerable distress and makes it hard to go about your day-to-day life.

The depressed mood must last for at least two weeks to qualify as major depression.

Certain medical conditions can cause symptoms similar to those of depression. Examples include thyroid disease, head injuries, anemia, mononucleosis, Lyme disease, chronic fatigue syndrome, and hepatitis. Some medications also can cause depression-like side effects. Alcohol or drug abuse can lead to depression, too. These other possibilities are ruled out first before depression is diagnosed. Of course, a constantly low mood is a problem that needs attention, no matter what the cause. But it's only major depression if the symptoms *aren't* due to the direct physical effects of a medical condition, a medication side effect, or substance abuse.

Signs and Symptoms

Along with making you feel sad, irritable, or apathetic, depression leads to a number of other symptoms. In my experience, these other symptoms caused much of the suffering associated with the disease. They made it hard for me to accomplish even the simplest tasks, from getting out of bed in the morning to eating a meal to going to sleep at night.

Below are descriptions of the depression warning signs. If you're suffering from major depression, you might not have all these symptoms. However, you will have at least three or four in addition to a depressed mood. There's no such thing as a "typical" person with depression, since each individual is different. But I think you'll recognize many of my experiences in the symptoms below.

There's no such thing as a "typical" person with depression.

Changes in Eating Habits

People who are depressed often have an increase or decrease in appetite. As a result, they may gain too much weight, or they may lose a lot of weight without trying. For instance, a 120-pound person might unintentionally gain or lose more than five pounds in a single month. In my case, food seemed to lose all its flavor and appeal, and it was often all I could do to choke down a few bites.

Changes in Sleeping Habits

Many people with depression have insomnia, which means they have trouble falling or staying asleep. Or their sleep may be of such poor quality that they don't feel rested and refreshed the next morning. Others suffer from excessive sleepiness, known as hypersomnia. They may sleep too long at night, or they might have trouble staying alert and awake during the day. For me, insomnia was a constant battle. When I finally did get to sleep, nightmares often woke me up halfway through the night.

Changes in Activity Level

When people are depressed, their actions often seem either unusually keyed up or unnaturally slowed down. For example, a person might show keyed up behavior by pacing and fidgeting. A person might show slowed down behavior by dragging out their words and appearing to move in slow motion. For me, it felt like I was always trying to move through a vat of molasses.

It felt like I was always trying to move through a vat of molasses.

Changes in Energy Level

When I was depressed, I felt drained of energy and tired all the time. It seemed like my internal battery had run down, and no amount of rest could charge it up again. Such fatigue is another common symptom of depression. It's one of the most disabling and frustrating aspects of the disease.

Feelings of Worthlessness

People with depression often feel worthless or extremely guilty, even when there's no logical reason to feel this way. Taken to an extreme, they may wind up feeling personally responsible for things that are clearly out of their control, from a parent's drinking problem to the state of world hunger. In my case, I blamed myself for getting sick, and I took my symptoms as signs of personal failure.

Changes in Thinking Ability

Depression can impair people's ability to think clearly and make good choices. Some people who are depressed have trouble concentrating on what they're doing, often because thoughts of worthlessness or guilt keep getting in the way. Others feel mentally paralyzed, unable to make even basic decisions. Personally, I felt too mentally exhausted to think much of the time, and too preoccupied with depression to focus on anything else. My brain was as worn down by the disease as my body.

Thoughts of Suicide

Some people with depression have repeated thoughts of death and suicide. Unfortunately, I was one of them. Without treatment, such thoughts may progress from wishing to be dead, to

"I hate feeling this way. Why can't I just snap out of it?"

Depression is a brain disease, not a character flaw. You don't choose to have depression any more than you would choose to have allergies, cancer, or epilepsy. Since you didn't become sick by choice, you can't simply wish your symptoms away. Fortunately, you *can* help yourself feel better by getting appropriate treatment. It's not magic, but it is a realistic way to take charge of your mental health.

thinking that others would be better off if you died, to making suicide plans, to putting the plans into action. Suicidal behavior is the most serious, irreversible consequence of depression, so this symptom should always be taken seriously. If you're having repeated thoughts about wanting to die, *get help right away*. For more information about handling suicidal thoughts and feelings, see Chapter 3.

Depression Plus Another Disorder

For depressed teens, having at least one other disorder is the rule rather than the exception.

Depression alone is bad enough. But many people with depression also have other emotional, behavioral, or learning disorders to contend with. In fact, for depressed teens, having at least one other disorder is the rule rather than the exception. The term "comorbidity" is psych lingo for the presence of two or more disorders at once in the same person. Below are some conditions that may exist side by side with depression:

- Anxiety disorders—Everyone feels a little nervous or worried at times. But for those with an anxiety disorder, the fear or worry is so overwhelming that it interferes with

Guy's-Eye View

On paper, depression and anxiety disorders can be neatly divided into their separate boxes. When these disorders are all jumbled up in a real, live human being, however, the boundaries between them become much less clear. It's often hard to tell where one disorder ends and another begins.

Jake is a case in point. As a 19-year-old college sophomore, he's doing quite well. But a year ago, it was a different story. "Toward the end of my first semester at college, I sank into a deep depression," he says. "I wound up just lying in bed staring at the ceiling tiles. I didn't want to move, I didn't sleep for three days, and I lost all interest in eating. I'm 5'10", and I was down to 102 pounds. Finals were right around the corner, and there was a dark pain in my stomach that wouldn't go away."

Around this time, Jake also began having panic attacks—sudden, unexpected waves of intense fear that are accompanied by physical signs of anxiety, such as a racing heart, shortness of breath, or sweating. Jake says, "The depression had sent me into a state of hopelessness and helplessness. I was afraid I could never feel happy again. I think it was this nonstop fear that set off my first panic attack. After the first attack, though, anything could set off another one—having trouble catching my breath, being in a closed space, having a stomachache. And the more aware I became of my depression, the more panic attacks I had, which only made me feel worse about myself." So the depression fed the anxiety, which fed the depression in turn.

Fortunately, Jake *was* able to feel happy again with the help of medication and psychotherapy to treat both the depression and the anxiety. In the process, he learned a lot about depression, and he realized how common it was. To share what he had learned with others, he started a campus group for other students in similar situations. Says Jake, "The problem is people don't talk about depression, so you end up thinking you're crazy. What really helped me was knowing there were other people out there who had been through the same things and knew what I was feeling."

their ability to get along in everyday life. Anxiety disorders come in several forms, but they all involve excessive fear or worry that either lasts a long time or recurs again and again. More than 60% of depressed teens have had an anxiety disorder, either in the past or at the same time as their depression.

- Substance abuse—It's not uncommon for people with depression to try relieving their pain by abusing alcohol or other drugs. Inevitably, they just end up making themselves feel worse. Plus, they may create a whole host of new problems for themselves while under the influence—by getting arrested, having car accidents, putting themselves in dangerous situations, or making risky choices about sexual behavior. Cigarette smoking is often associated with depression as well.
- Eating disorders—We live in a society that's obsessed with food and weight. However, people who suffer from eating disorders are compelled to act on these obsessions to a destructive extreme. Some severely restrict what they eat, at times to the point of self-starvation. Others go on eating binges, then try to compensate by means such as self-induced vomiting or misuse of laxatives. From one-third to one-half of all people with eating disorders also suffer from some form of depression.
- Attention-deficit hyperactivity disorder (ADHD)—All of us occasionally drift into daydreams, squirm in our seat, or leap before we look. But for those with ADHD, this type of behavior is so frequent and extreme that it causes major disruption in their lives. Some people with ADHD are easily distracted and have trouble paying attention to anything for very long. Others are overly active and im-

pulsive. They may bounce out of their chair, talk too much, act without thinking, and blurt out the first thing that crosses their mind. Still other people have both these kinds of symptoms combined. It's not uncommon for adolescents with depression to also have ADHD.

- Conduct disorder—I'm the first to admit that testing the rules a little bit is part of being a teenager. But some teens take this so far that they do serious harm to themselves or others. They have trouble following *any* rules at all. These are teens who threaten others, get into physical fights, set fires, vandalize property, lie to their friends, steal from their parents, stay out all night, or run away from home. Conduct disorder and depression often go hand in hand.
- Learning disorders—A learning disorder adversely affects a person's performance in school or ability to function in everyday situations that call for reading, writing, or math. Depression itself can make it difficult for students to focus in class, and it can sap them of the energy and motivation they need to study. As a result, grades often sink along with their mood. When you add a learning disorder to the mix, the situation becomes even more challenging. Getting back on track at school may take not only treatment but also classroom adjustments.

To obtain more information about these disorders, see the "Help for Related Problems" section in the Resources near the end of this book. Depression plus another disorder can equal big trouble unless both conditions are diagnosed and treated properly. If you think you might be affected by another disorder in addition to depression, a trained mental health professional can help you sort out the problems.

Having two disorders just makes it doubly important to reach out for help when you're struggling. The good news is that treatment can help you feel better, even when your depression is severe or complicated by another disorder. If I had only understood that sooner, I could have saved myself and my family a lot of pain.

Treatment can help you feel better

Chapter Three

My Last Thread Pulled Apart: Thoughts of Suicide

My Story

This is the point in my story when I hit rock bottom—so it's ironic that this is also the point when help was finally on the way. I was waiting for an appointment with a highly recommended psychiatrist when a spot suddenly opened up in his schedule due to a patient's cancellation. Now I only had to wait one more day. Just 24 hours before I would receive the help I desperately needed. At last, maybe someone would be able to explain what was happening inside my head.

I had so many questions that sounded like distant echoes in my brain. Why were my mind and body slowly, systematically, shutting down? Where had all the joy in my life gone? And what was this dark void that had taken its place? Twenty-four hours may be only a day, but it can seem like an eternity when you feel as if you're barely hanging on by a slender thread.

When my mom hung up the phone with the secretary from the psychiatrist's office, I saw a flicker of hope in her eyes. At that moment, she had far more hope for me than I had for myself. She needed to believe that someone could save her daughter from slowly and quietly drifting away. I didn't realize it then, but my mom was functioning in a purely primal mode. She was like a mother lion. Her mission was to protect me and ensure my survival, no matter what she was up against. When I was younger, my mom had tried her best to keep me safe from the dangers of the outside world, and now she was literally protecting me from myself.

My mom believed that the best way to shield me from this internal enemy was to never lose sight of me. We talked about what we should do that day, but I really didn't have enough energy left to think about what I wanted. Honestly, I didn't *want* to do anything, because I had ceased caring about the things that made me feel alive. My mom did the thinking, and she thought we should go to the places that usually held some sort of revitalizing power for me.

Hanging on by a Thread

We spent most of the morning in the woods. Since I was very young, I have felt close to nature, and I've understood that I draw inner strength from being in natural places. We slowly walked a path that meandered through the forest. I remember looking up and outlining the shapes of the canopy in my mind. I spoke very little, because it took great effort and my words had begun to slur badly.

At one point, we rested for a few minutes on a bench beside the trail. I leaned back and felt the sun on my face, listened to bird songs, and savored the slight summer breeze on my bare arms. Closing my eyes, I thought about how therapeutic this peacefulness was. But then I remembered that soon I would be leaving the forest, and once again, I would be faced with a world where I felt too weak to survive. I kept this thought to myself, though, not wanting my mom to know about the morbid fears unfolding inside my mind. My depression seemed contagious, and I would never wish that kind of pain on anyone—especially not anyone I loved.

After we left the forest, my mom suggested that the best place to go next would be a movie theater. For a long time, my mom and I have been avid cinema fans. Usually, we would pick an obscure film at the independent theater, because we liked to go to a movie without knowing much about it. On that day, though, we decided to see a mainstream comedy. I don't remember much about the movie itself; depression was consuming all my attention by that point. But I do recall my mom and myself sitting silently in the back row while the theater was erupting with laughter. I didn't care about the punch lines and inane plot, and my mom was just burning away the hours until the next morning.

After the movie, my mom suggested that we eat at one of our favorite Italian restaurants, where they make the best comfort food in town. The owners have decorated the restaurant in a Beatles theme, so the atmosphere there is unique and fun. But I might as well have been eating mush in a stark, white room. It was all the same to me. I could barely fit any food into my shrunken stomach anyway, and I had lost all pleasure in the flavor. My taste buds had faded away, just like the rest of me.

Sitting there with my mom in the "Octopus Garden," I listened to her tell me that I was going to make it until tomorrow, that I just needed to hang on a little bit longer. She kept saying that she was right by my side. Her face looked so tired from the constant strain of worrying about me. But although she was scared and exhausted, she tried to take on some of my pain so I wouldn't have to bear the full load. My mom wanted more than anything to support me in my struggle. Yet even with that kind of love in my life, I still felt lost and alone.

When we got home that evening, I actually felt as if I could sleep. I was so worn down, mentally and physically, that I was willing to face the recurring nightmares that visited me nearly every night. I went upstairs to my room and mechanically climbed into bed. I didn't go through my entire bedtime routine—dental hygiene was the furthest thing from my mind. All I wanted to do was sleep and then wake up. My goals had become very basic.

Alone in the Night

The house was quiet. My mom was finishing up some chores in the kitchen before coming upstairs to tell me goodnight. I was 14, and I needed my mom to tuck me in. I felt like a helpless child seeking comfort wherever I could—yet more evidence that seemed to reaffirm my weakness.

My dad was outside working on one of our broken-down cars. It was growing late, and mosquitoes were swarming around his light, but he still put off coming inside the emotionally charged house. My dad worked hard to avoid facing the problems that I was struggling with, because they were too much like his own. When he interacted with me, I was like a mirror that reflected his own low-lying depression. Everyone has his own way of coping with things, and my dad's way was to stay emotionally and physically distant.

My brother was out with his friends. He was 16 and it was summer, so he was rarely home. I didn't realize it at the time, but it hurt him to have our family and friends pay so much more attention to me. He didn't believe that I was truly sick, but thought it was a ploy to monopolize everyone's time. Like my dad, but for different reasons, my brother kept his distance.

In my bedroom, I was looking in the mirror at a person I didn't recognize anymore. I feared that I would look like this empty shell forever. When my mom finally came into my room, I crawled into bed, and she gently pulled the covers over me and caressed my cheek. She said she loved me more than anything and would never give up on helping me.

I was looking in the mirror at a person I didn't recognize anymore.

After she left, I began to think about when I was young. I was worried about being kidnapped, and I asked my mom over and over if she would look for me if I were missing. She always replied that she would never stop looking, and I believe she felt the same way about this situation. I still trusted her through all of the paranoid thoughts of abandonment and the heavy feeling of hopelessness. She sat with me for a few minutes and then said goodnight. On her way out, she said she was staying up awhile, and to let her know if I needed anything. Then she turned off the light and closed the door, leaving it slightly ajar.

I lay awake in bed looking at the small beam of light pushing from the hallway through the crack in the door. I related to that light, a narrow beam surrounded by vast darkness. A swell of unbridled sadness climbed out of my stomach and up into my throat, and I began to cry. I remained silent as I felt one tear after another stream down my cheek. The tears were unstoppable, and soon there was a large, wet stain on my pillow. At that point, I felt certain that the psychiatrist wouldn't be able to help me. How could anyone understand this kind of pain, invisible and locked away within the recesses of my brain? I felt that no one else on earth could possibly have experienced what I was going through then.

The Thread Snaps

Everyone has their last thread—their final, tenuous connection to life. For me, it was the knowledge that it would break the hearts of my loved ones if I were to die. Especially my mom. She would be shattered into an infinite number of pieces, and I couldn't bear to destroy her that way. But for the first time, I began to wonder whether my loved ones might actually be better off if I weren't around to poison their lives with my toxic gloom. Maybe my mom wouldn't shatter at all—maybe she would be much happier instead.

It was only a few weeks before that I had first considered suicide as a legitimate solution to my problems. Now my last reason for living was fast slipping away. My love for family and friends was no longer strong enough to battle the irrational thoughts that were tumbling through my brain. My last thread pulled apart. My spirit instantly flooded with enough hopelessness to make me feel mortally wounded. I wanted to die. I needed to end this pain now.

My mind was made up. Suddenly, with an eerie calm, my body was ready to join the spirit that had died weeks before. I felt like a preprogrammed robot as I swung my legs out of bed. I walked across the room to my art desk. With strange detachment, I thought of the many creative moments I had spent at this desk. Now it was only the place where I was choosing to die.

I clicked on the desk lamp and reached for my box of carving knives. Inside the box were two handles and a row of differently shaped X-acto blades. My art supplies had become my means of self-destruction. In retrospect, our lack of knowledge about depression was what kept all these tools within easy reach. When I picked up one of the knives, I believed that I was making a logical choice, but my "logic" was far from rational at that moment. The metal handle felt cool and dry in my sweaty palm, and all awareness of the outside world slipped away.

You might say that what happened next was divine intervention, mother's intuition, or just dumb luck. But right at that moment, my mom walked to the foot of the stairs and called up to me. She asked if I was all right, because she knew I had been having trouble sleeping. She had stayed up late because she couldn't sleep either.

Her voice cut through the darkness and struck me so hard that I was knocked back into reality. Suddenly, seeing what I was about to do, I was filled with fear and self-loathing. With a shaky voice, I lied and called back that I was okay. But in truth, I was utterly terrified. For a moment, I had welcomed and accepted suicide. It's extremely unnerving to realize that you have managed to outwit the basic human instinct telling you to do whatever is necessary to survive.

I turned off the desk lamp and quietly climbed back into bed. My body would not stop trembling, and I felt queasy. As on so many other nights, sleep did not come. But I remained there, secure in my bed, as the final hours until morning ticked away.

The Big Picture

I made it back from the edge that night, but tragically, some are not so fortunate. In the United States, suicide is the third leading cause of death among people between the ages of 15 and 24. Within this group, the risk just increases with age. People in their early twenties are 50% more likely to die from suicide than those in their late teens.

I made it back from the edge that night.

Young males are almost six times as likely as females to die from suicide. Yet females attempt it more often. The choice of method may help explain this difference. Females are more likely to take an overdose, and there is a greater chance of being rescued from self-poisoning than from a gunshot. However, there

Guy's-Eye View

"At 16, my anthem was, 'I wish I had never been born,'" says Adam. The words were stuck in his head like an annoying song you wish you could forget, but can't. Although he never acted on his suicidal impulses, Adam says he thought about suicide often. Around the same time, Adam also became obsessed with fantasy novels and TV shows. "Hey, why couldn't *I* be a supernatural crime fighter? I really wanted to be anyone but who I was and anywhere but in my own life."

As Adam's depression grew worse, the former star student all but stopped going to school. "It got so bad that I was missing three or four days a week," he says. "I quit caring about school—it seemed so trivial compared to other things going on in my life." Among those things was a custody dispute between his divorced parents. "I had supervised visits with my dad for an hour at a time, a couple of nights a month," Adam says. "My dad had beat me up pretty badly at one point, and after that, the court wouldn't allow him to see me alone." Adam began refusing to go to the visits, just as he was refusing to go to school, so his dad asked the court to intervene.

As part of the process, the court recommended that Adam be evaluated by a psychologist. It was this psychologist who first recognized that Adam's problems were actually symptoms of depression. Adam began psychotherapy, and shortly afterward, he started taking medication as well. The depression didn't vanish immediately, but the suicidal thoughts went away, and the other symptoms lessened enough for him to start tackling the all-important work of feeling better again.

"If you're having suicidal thoughts, confide in someone you trust," says Adam, now a 22-year-old junior at an Ivy League university. "Make sure someone else knows so preventive measures can be taken, if needed. And since such thoughts are a clear sign that something is seriously wrong, they warrant a trip to a psychologist or psychiatrist." Give yourself a chance to see how the story of your life is going to turn out. When you've reached the darkest point, you know it can only get better.

Give yourself a chance to see how the story of your life is going to turn out.

doesn't seem to be any difference between the sexes when it comes to the seriousness of their intent. In countries with few medical resources for treating poisonings, women actually die by suicide more often than men.

Suicidal thoughts are even more common than actions. According to survey data from the Centers for Disease Control and Prevention, about one in every six high school students has seriously considered suicide within the past year. Such thoughts are often closely intertwined with the confused thinking of mental illness. Looking back, I realize how irrational it was to consider hurting myself. But in my fog of total hopelessness at the time, death was the only option I could see—my mind was completely closed to other, far superior alternatives.

One in every six high school students has seriously considered suicide within the past year.

I was thinking under the influence of depression. While most people with depression don't become suicidal, a significant minority do. In fact, about two-thirds of all people who die by suicide have some type of depressive disorder. The combination of depression and substance abuse can be particularly lethal. In addition, studies have shown that the risk of suicide goes up when depression is mixed with feelings of anxiety, aggression, or agitation.

If you have ever doubted whether depression is a "real" illness, consider this: Left untreated, depression can be fatal. When dying starts to seem more attractive than living, that's your cue to get help immediately. Admitting that you are suicidal may be one of the hardest things you will ever have to do. In my case, I felt a burning shame and utter terror whenever I thought about what I had almost done. I saw myself as weak, and I knew that acknowledging suicidal tendencies would mean that

I had to tackle the enormous mountain called recovery. The task seemed insurmountable. Yet as difficult as it was to reach out for help, the effort was well worth it. I'm still here and enjoying life again—that's all the proof I need.

I knew that acknowledging suicidal tendencies would mean that I had to tackle the enormous mountain called recovery.

Warning Signs to Watch For

My own brush with suicide came when I reached my early teens. For the first time, I was starting to steer my own life, but I still didn't know exactly where I wanted to go. It was a scary, out-of-control feeling—chances are, you've felt it at some point, too. A certain amount of stress, confusion, self-doubt, or uncertainty about the future is only natural as you head into adulthood. But following are some warning signs that you might be cruising for an emotional crash:

- Feeling hopeless about the future
- Thinking of yourself as a bad or worthless person
- Being unable to tolerate praise
- Withdrawing from family, friends, and activities
- Neglecting your personal appearance
- Feeling constantly bored or unable to concentrate
- Letting your schoolwork slide
- Abusing alcohol or other drugs
- Getting involved in violent or dangerous situations
- Dwelling on repeated thoughts of death or suicide
- Developing a specific suicide plan
- Having other symptoms of depression (see Chapter 2)

If you recognize these signs in yourself, don't wait for a suicidal crisis. Get help sooner rather than later. At the very least,

Suicide Prevention Hotlines

These national, 24-hour hotlines can provide immediate assistance if you're thinking about suicide:

- National Hopeline Network, 1-800-SUICIDE (784-2433)
- National Suicide Prevention Lifeline, 1-800-273-TALK (8255)

you'll save yourself from needless suffering. At most, you might actually save your own life.

Risk Factors for Suicide

Certain other factors also tend to increase the risk of suicide. Keep in mind, though, that most people with these characteristics never become suicidal. These are simply clues that you might be a bit more vulnerable than average. Just because you have one or more risk factors doesn't automatically mean you'll have suicidal thoughts, and just because you're free of risk factors doesn't mean you won't.

Personal risk factors

- Depression, substance abuse, or other mental illness
- Impulsive or aggressive tendencies
- Past experience with trauma or abuse
- Previous suicide attempt
- Family history of suicide

Environmental risk factors

- Loss of a key relationship or social role
- Easy access to guns or other lethal methods of suicide
- Stigma attached to seeking help
- Lack of access to mental health care
- Media reports that glamorize suicide

Obviously, you can't catch suicide the way you do a cold or the flu. But suicide can be "contagious" in the sense that knowing or hearing about others who have died of suicide may influence you when you're vulnerable. Be very skeptical of attempts to portray suicide as romantic or heroic. In truth, it's a harsh, destructive, permanent solution to a temporary problem.

Be very skeptical of attempts to portray suicide as romantic or heroic.

By the way, it's a myth that if you talk about suicide you won't really do it. In fact, many people who attempt suicide do confide in someone first. The more you find yourself talking, writing, and thinking about suicide, the louder the alarm bells should be sounding in your brain.

Often, a stressful event is the last straw that actually sets a suicide in motion. This may involve some type of rejection or disappointment, such as fighting with a parent, breaking up with a girlfriend or boyfriend, or not getting into the college of your dreams. Of course, the vast majority of people who have such setbacks don't become suicidal. They feel lousy for a while, and then they bounce back. But when the stress is added on top of another problem, such as depression, it can be tougher to handle. For some people, this sets off a downward spiral.

What to Do if You're Suicidal

If suicide ever starts to seem like a logical option, *tell someone you trust.* Ideally, this should be a person who will listen to you, understand the gravity of the situation, and help you figure out what to do next. Choose someone who treats you well and has your best interests at heart. As a general rule, it may be better to choose an older person—such as a parent or another

"My friend has confided that he's thinking about suicide. How can I help?"

If a friend says he is thinking about suicide, always take it seriously. Listen calmly without judging. Then offer concrete suggestions for finding professional help. Share the hotline numbers in this chapter, or pass on the name of a doctor, therapist, counselor, or other professional who has been helpful to you. If you think it might help, offer to go along to the first visit for moral support.

In some cases, you may believe that your friend is in imminent danger of hurting himself. Don't try to handle such a volatile situation on your own. Instead, get help immediately, even if the other person asks you not to. Call your friend's parents and let them know it's an emergency, or simply dial 911. Then don't leave your friend alone until help arrives. You're not betraying his trust by breaking a confidence in this situation. To the contrary, you just might be saving his life.

older relative—who has more experience to draw upon when handling a crisis situation.

Keep in mind, though, that even the most sympathetic, well-meaning family members and friends may not know much about suicide and depression. They also may be so overwhelmed by their own fear, worry, and guilt that they're unable to think clearly and react appropriately. Some might minimize your feelings or question how real they are. Others might show a lack of understanding about depression by criticizing, judging, ridiculing, or blaming you. Don't let this type of unhelpful response keep you from getting the assistance you need.

Because suicidal thoughts are an urgent problem, you also need to *seek professional help right away.* If you're already in treatment for depression, call your psychiatrist or therapist. If not, a parent, doctor, counselor, school nurse, or religious adviser may be able to help you find a mental health care provider.

Depression creates an illusion of total despair, and this illusion grows in intensity when you isolate yourself and stew in it.

If you ever feel as if you're ready to act on a suicidal impulse, *don't let yourself be alone.* Depression creates an illusion of total despair, and this illusion grows in intensity when you isolate yourself and stew in it. On the night when I hit my lowest point, I was in my bedroom, only one floor above my mom. I was in the same house, but I felt miles apart. I had just enough time alone in my room to conclude that my life wasn't going to improve and therefore it was time to stop living.

When you're in a suicidal crisis, everything inside of you may be insisting that you are alone. Don't believe it. There are people out there who want to help, if you just give them a chance. You also may find a little comfort in knowing that so many others have fallen into the depths of depression. Like me, most have discovered that once you hit rock bottom, there's nowhere left to go but up.

Chapter Four

Eight Days in the Dark: A Stay in the Hospital

My Story

The next morning, I had my scheduled appointment with the psychiatrist. My mom was unaware of the low point I had hit the night before, and I had no desire to tell her. I didn't want to cause her pain. Besides, by that time, I didn't have enough energy left to form words or string them together into coherent thoughts.

My mom did the talking as we drove into the city. Meanwhile, I stared out the window at the people passing by in cars or walking down the sidewalks. How could they stand this sad, gray world? I was living in a shadow, and I didn't understand how other people could act as if they were living in the light.

Meeting Dr. M.

The psychiatrist's office was located in a large building with glass windows on three sides. Entering the lobby, we found the psychiatrist's name on the board and walked upstairs to his second-floor office. Once in the waiting room, we sat with a handful of other patients and family members. Searching their faces, I wondered why they were there. Did anyone feel as low as I did? I sincerely doubted it.

Finally, the receptionist slid open the glass partition over her desk and called my name. I was to see the psychiatrist alone, while my mom filled out paperwork in the waiting room. Dr. M. met me in the hallway and shook my hand. As we walked toward his office, he made small talk to break the ice, but I didn't contribute much to the "getting to know you" conversation.

Yet even in my dour mood, I liked Dr. M. right away. He wore glasses, a colorful tie, and a gentle expression on his face. After we had settled into our seats in the office, Dr. M. opened a new file folder and began asking questions about my background. He wrote vigorously as I answered. Later, I learned that some of the characteristics he noted were my slurred speech, pale complexion, and vision problems. But at the time, I was just aware of the effort it took to respond.

Then the tone of the conversation shifted as the questions became more general. Dr. M. asked me what the date was; I didn't know. He asked me who the president was; I couldn't remember. He asked me to read a paragraph, and I could barely comprehend the words. The more questions he asked, the more I began to feel as if the purpose must be to see just how far gone I really was.

Finally, Dr. M. asked me to describe what was going on inside my head. Before I knew it, I was telling him about what had happened the previous night. I surprised even myself by how readily I gave up the information. When I look back at that moment, I believe that a basic survival instinct must have prompted me to reveal my secret. For the moment anyway, this instinct overrode my dark logic, and I spilled my story, not leaving out a single detail.

Dr. M. kept writing as I spoke, and the sound of his pen scratching the paper echoed within my brain. At last, he stopped writing and paged the secretary to send in my mom. Now it was my turn to sit in the waiting room while he spoke to her privately. As I left the office, I remember thinking how serious he looked. *I'm unfixable*, I thought, as I took a seat in the waiting room. I felt as if I could have fallen asleep right there and stayed that way forever.

I'm unfixable, I thought.

Eventually, I learned more about the conversation between the psychiatrist and my mom that day. Dr. M. recommended immediate action. His main concern was that I stay safe from myself, and he felt that the safest place for me at that point was a psychiatric hospital. My mom tried to explain the kind of person I used to be, but hearing how radically my behavior had changed only raised Dr. M.'s level of concern. He felt that medical testing and treatment should begin right away, so the plans were set in motion. I would stay in the hospital until some answers had been found and I felt well enough to trust myself again. Because my situation was so serious, my mom had no time to waste in getting me admitted into a hospital; she ended up deciding to check me into an inpatient psychiatric facility that my doctors had recommended.

Several minutes later, I was called back into the psychiatrist's office, and they told me about the plan. I could see that my mom was doing everything in her power to hold herself together. For my part, I was instantly struck by extreme sadness and bitter fear. My illness had officially evolved to another level. The depth of my depression had been acknowledged by one of the state's top psychiatrists, and I was going to get intensive treatment. There should have been some comfort in that, but instead there was just uncertainty and anxiety.

Next Stop: Mental Ward

My mom and I returned home so that I could pack a few belongings for the hospital stay. My memory from the time we left the psychiatrist's office to the time I checked into the hospital is hazy. But I know that I never put up a fight about going into the hospital. It takes passion to fight, and I was much too lethargic to care. As far as I was concerned, nothing mattered anymore.

It takes passion to fight, and I was much too lethargic to care.

At home, my mom helped me pack. While I was getting clothes together, she wrote a note of encouragement that I could take with me. The psychiatrist had warned her that I wouldn't be able to have any outside contact for at least 24 hours, so she wanted to make sure I had the note for moral support.

Our drive to the hospital was somber compared to other drives in the past. When we finally pulled into the hospital parking lot, my heart began racing nervously. But as we approached the building, I was surprised by how ordinary it looked. I don't know what I had expected—maybe something stark white, sterile, and intimidating? Instead, the lobby had an atrium with plants, tropical flowers, birds, and a waterfall. Maybe this tranquil-looking place wasn't going to be so bad after all. Maybe it would be a good place to rest. *I could use a rest,* I thought. *I'm so tired all the time.*

We were directed to a pair of double doors, where we waited for a nurse to buzz us in. As we walked through the doors, the atmosphere—and my thoughts—changed completely. This was closer to what I had expected. The main room of the adolescent unit was lit with harsh fluorescent light that bleached out the already-pale blue of the walls. To my left was a communal area, empty at the time, that held a stereo and TV locked in a

Plexiglas box. The area was furnished with big, block-shaped, blue vinyl chairs—the kind of furniture that an enraged patient couldn't easily use as a weapon. To my right was a small dining area set aside for those who, for whatever reason, weren't able to eat in the main cafeteria. Straight ahead was a station for the staff. It consisted of a smaller room made mostly of Plexiglas. Inside this small room were the electronic controls for the facility's locks and surveillance system.

This station was my first stop. The time had come to say goodbye to my mom. I was trying hard not to cry, because I didn't want her to see how truly scared I was. In retrospect, I think my mom was doing the same thing. She hugged me tightly, reminded me about the note, then turned to leave. Meanwhile, one of the nurses was inspecting my bag, looking for anything I could conceivably use to cause harm to myself or others. When the bag was returned, my sketchbook with the spiral binding and my art pencils and pens had been removed.

Next I got the rundown of rules and expectations: No unauthorized books, music, or phone calls. A rigid schedule with little personal time. A seemingly endless round of appointments for assessments and therapy. My head was spinning as the staff person talked about hospital routine. I was still replaying the memory of watching my mom walk away. It was dawning on me that this probably was not going to be a great place for rest and relaxation.

After that, I was led to a set of doors on the other side of the room. The staff person and I were buzzed through, and we entered an area with three hallways leading in different directions. This, I learned, was the section of the unit reserved for people who were under suicide watch. I would be escorted to and from my room by a staff member at all times. Other than that, I would have no contact with anyone else in the unit as long as I was deemed a suicide risk.

When we reached my room, I was told to settle in for the evening. Someone would come and retrieve me at 7:00 the next morning. Then the staff person left, locking the door from the outside. I put down my bag and sat on the bed, listening to the silence. The sun was starting to set, and it gave the white room an orangey glow. I was feeling as low and empty as I had the night before.

Yet this night, I fell asleep almost as soon as my head hit the pillow. A few hours later, I awoke to a bad dream and had trouble falling back asleep again. Lying there in the dark, I would hear a key jiggling in the lock on my door about every half hour. The door would open briefly, letting in a shaft of light, then quietly close. They were checking to make sure I hadn't found a way to do myself in. Every time the door opened, I pretended that I was sleeping. I didn't want to have to talk to anyone. After a couple of hours, I finally drifted off.

Lost in Space

The next morning, I awoke to the sound of someone entering my room. It was a different staff person explaining the schedule for the day. I was given five minutes to get dressed. Then a man appeared to escort me through the locked double doors and into the main room of the unit. As I was led to an exam room located off one side of the communal area, I saw a couple of other kids sitting in the big, blue chairs. They were looking me over intently, and I guessed that they must have been trying to figure out my reason for being there.

In the exam room, I sat on the examination table, and the same man who had escorted me there took my blood pressure. He explained that I would come here first thing every morning to have my vital signs checked. While he was taking my blood pressure, he asked all kinds of questions about my bodily functions. I felt strange telling someone in detail about what I had left in the toilet, but he told me it was important to monitor my physical health.

After a slew of personal questions, I was led to the small, solitary dining area. I would have breakfast there by myself, away from the other patients. I managed to force down a small amount of food, but it gave me no pleasure. Then it was time to begin a full day of testing.

First up was a battery of psychological tests. I was led out of the adolescent unit to another part of the hospital, where I was handed over to a doctor I had never met before. I did poorly on the IQ portion. I couldn't even piece words together, and I was being asked to jump through intellectual hoops. The inkblot test went a little better, but it was still grueling. The questions seemed endless, and my mind began to stray further and further from the task at hand. I was getting very tired of this stranger's demands to know the ins and outs of my intimate thoughts.

After that came the medical testing. For the next couple of hours, I was examined from head to toe. The doctors needed to rule out other medical conditions that could be causing my symptoms. It makes sense now, but at the time, all I knew was that they were poking around at me while I was lying on a table. I had felt mentally exposed before, and now nothing about me remained private.

Eventually, I emerged from the exam room and was taken back to the adolescent unit for lunch. I was scheduled to meet with my psychiatrist in the afternoon. Even though I had only recently met Dr. M., it was good to see a face I recognized. We sat at one of the tables in the empty lounge, and we talked about the medication I would start taking once all the testing was completed. As Dr. M. was getting up to leave, he mentioned that the newer depression medications were safer than the older ones. At first, I thought he was referring just to side effects, but I was wrong. He added that overdosing with the newer medications was nearly impossible. *He probably doesn't impart that information to everyone*, I thought. Once again, I felt singled out. I was a damaged and unpredictable patient.

I missed how I used to be, and I wondered if I would ever be back to my old self again.

After an isolated dinner in the small dining area, I was escorted back to my room. Once there, I began to cry inconsolably. I missed my home, I missed my family and friends, I missed my pets. But most of all, I missed how I used to be, and I wondered if I would ever be back to my old self again.

Off Suicide Watch

More testing followed on my second full day in the hospital. On the third day, I was finally taken off suicide watch. Now I wouldn't have to be checked constantly while I was trying to sleep. Even better, I could receive mail and phone calls from family members, and my mom would be able to visit that afternoon. Plus, I would be allowed to join the general population on the ward, where I could interact with other patients at meals and during free time.

That morning, I talked to my mom on the phone, and I had never been happier to hear her voice. By early afternoon, I had received a number of cards and flowers from well-wishers. It seemed that word had traveled fast about my condition. Everyone had seen how quickly I was sinking, and there was a wave of relief when they heard that I was getting professional help.

Each card from family and friends dripped with emotion—shock, fear, sadness, love, encouragement.

Among the letters was one from my dad. It was always easier for him to express himself in writing rather than face to face. In his letter, my dad apologized for his absence, emotionally speaking, throughout this ordeal. He told me how afraid he felt when he realized how much I was struggling. It felt really good to know that he cared. I had thought he was keeping his distance because of indifference, but he was actually avoiding his own issues with depression. I reminded him too much of himself.

Later that afternoon, I had my first group counseling session with two other patients. The counselor introduced us all to each other. Then we took turns explaining how we landed in this place. The first to speak was a 13-year-old boy who was on his third hospitalization within a year. He spoke with a lot of energy and force, and he had trouble sitting still. As he talked, his eyes and thoughts darted around, unable to focus on anything for long. The more he spoke, the more I could see how lonely he felt. I could picture him sitting in his parents' large, luxurious home in a wealthy neighborhood. He had everything but no one to share it with.

The next to speak was a girl my age who had grown up living with her mom and her mom's various boyfriends. From a young age, she had been sexually and physically abused. This girl had been around violence and drugs all her life. She told one particularly harrowing story about a time when her mom was threatened with a gun and used her as a shield. By the time she was 11, she had developed a drug problem herself and stopped going to school. This was her fifth time in the hospital. She saw her life as completely worthless.

After this incredibly sad and disturbing story, it was my turn to talk. I was at a loss for words. I couldn't explain why I was there. I hadn't been abused or neglected. I didn't have any substance abuse problems. I lived in a loving, middle-class home, and I had received an outpouring of support from my large network of family and friends. I began to feel frustrated, because I couldn't find a convenient explanation for my depression. I was just depressed, and that was that.

I felt a little embarrassed and even unworthy telling my story to the group. But the others listened with attention and respect. Looking back, there seemed to be an underlying empathy among the patients. People honored each other's stories. We had all been laid low by our illnesses, and that was a common thread tying us together, no matter how different other parts of our lives seemed.

There seemed to be an underlying empathy among the patients. People honored each other's stories.

Homeward Bound

The next few days passed slowly. I had gotten my art supplies back, so I drew in my free time. I discovered that I could articulate how I felt much louder and more clearly through my drawings than through my words. Often, other kids in the adolescent unit would watch me draw. Then suddenly they would open up, telling me intimate details of their lives almost like they were in confession. I think they felt comfortable sharing their private thoughts and feelings with me because they knew I would understand. Their pain was right there in the pages of my sketchbook.

On the fifth day, I met with one of the staff counselors to draw up an action plan for coping with depression after I was discharged. The counselor was determined that I pinpoint a solid source of trouble in my life and then figure out how I was going to deal with it once I returned to the "real world." I searched my mind, trying to find a neat explanation for my pain. Just feeling sad clearly wasn't going to be enough. All I could think of was my not-so-good relationship with my dad. Even then, I knew it wasn't the sole cause of my depression. I had to say something, because I wanted the counselor to think I was making progress. In the back of my mind, though, I kept thinking about all the horror stories she must have heard. To me, an emotionally distant dad sounded extremely low on the scale of life problems.

Afterward, I had some free time in my schedule. It was still hard for me to write, but nevertheless I decided to tackle several worksheets I had been given to fill out. *The sooner I get these done, the sooner I can leave*, I thought. I had only been in the hospital five days, but it felt much longer. I was tired of staying in the same building all the time, cut off from everyone and everything I loved. I wanted to sleep in my own bed, and when I woke up, I wanted to be outside in the summer sun. Then it dawned on me: I was caring about things again. Even though my thoughts remained largely negative, I was starting to remember the positives in my life as well.

Even though my thoughts remained largely negative, I was starting to remember the positives in my life as well.

By the eighth day, I was ready to be discharged. This time, when I was buzzed through the doors, my mom was waiting on the other side. I embraced her, and she held my arm as we walked out of the building. When I got into passenger side of the car, I let out a long sigh of relief. I felt as if I had aged years during those days in the hospital, but now I was going home. And for the first time in weeks, I was catching a glimpse of sunlight behind the clouds.

The Big Picture

While I had briefly hoped that my stay in a psychiatric hospital might be like a week at camp, I soon learned otherwise. My experiences there were alternately disorienting, frustrating, and exhausting. Ultimately, though, the hospital gave me a safe place to catch my breath and regain my footing. Although a stint in a psychiatric hospital is no one's first choice for treatment, I realize now that it was the best option for me at the time.

Hospitalization involves inpatient treatment in a facility that provides intensive, specialized care and close, round-the-clock monitoring. It's the most restrictive level of care, and therefore it's the one reserved for the most severe or highest risk cases. Most people with depression never need hospitalization. For those like me who do, however, it offers a chance to work on suicidal feelings or severe symptoms in a safe, controlled setting.

Decisions about hospitalization are made on a case-by-case basis. As examples, though, a hospital stay might be recommended if you:

- Pose a threat to yourself or others
- Are behaving in a bizarre or destructive manner
- Require medication that must be closely monitored for a while
- Need round-the-clock care to get your symptoms under control
- Have not improved in treatment outside the hospital

Testing, Testing

Before psychiatric treatment in a hospital begins, you will need to undergo a thorough evaluation. As I found out, this can be a rather rigorous and lengthy process. A typical evaluation includes several components:

Many artists are known to have had periods of depression. The art shown here is by artists who probably knew what it felt like to be depressed.

Among the Firs, by Canadian artist Emily Carr (1871–1945).
Collection of Glenbow Museum [56.2.2], Calgary, Canada.

Wanderer Above a Sea of Fog, by German artist Caspar David Friedrich (1774–1840).
Hamburger Kunsthalle, Hamburg, Germany. Bildarchiv Preussischer Kulturbesitz/Art Resource, New York.

Untitled, by a 14-year-old American girl (1993).
From *Childhood Revealed: Art Expressing Pain, Discovery, and Hope.*
New York University Child Study Center, by permission.

Moon Animal, by American artist William Baziotes (1912–1963). *Festival of Arts Purchase, Krannert Art Museum and Kinkead Pavilion, University of Illinois, Urbana-Champaign, 1951-6-1.*

Untitled, by contemporary American artist Lucia Ballester. National Art Exhibitions by the Mentally Ill.

Untitled, by American artist Franz Kline (1910–1962). Hirshhorn Museum and Sculpture Garden, Smithsonian Institution, Gift of Joseph H. Hirshhorn, 1966. © 2006 The Franz Kline Estate / Artists Rights Society (ARS), New York.

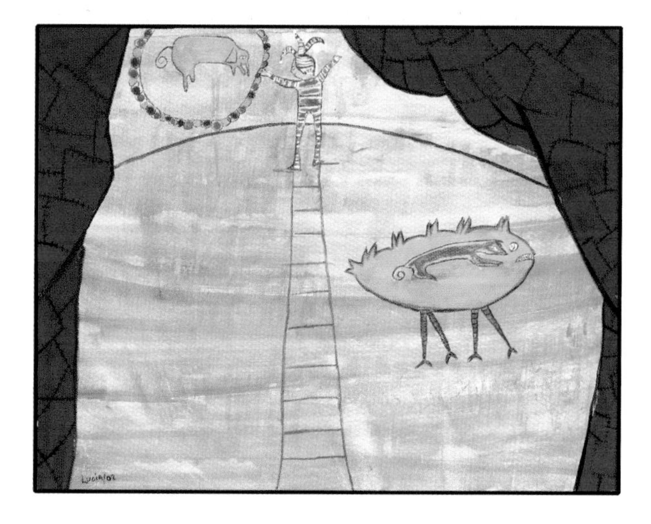

Untitled, by contemporary American artist Lucia Ballester. National Art Exhibitions by the Mentally Ill.

Untitled, by author and artist Cait Irwin, at age 15.

On a Sailboat, by German artist Caspar David Friedrich (1774–1840). The State Hermitage Museum, St. Petersburg, Russia. Bridgeman-Giraudon/Art Resource, New York.

City Park That I Slept In, by contemporary American artist Roger Sadler. National Art Exhibitions by the Mentally Ill.

Ten Questions to Ask

The more you know about hospital treatment, the less scary and confusing it's likely to seem. If your psychiatrist recommends a short hospital stay, these are some questions you or your parents may want to ask:

- Why is inpatient treatment in a psychiatric hospital being recommended?
- Are there other alternatives for treatment, and if so, how do they compare?
- If you are hospitalized, what assessments and treatments will you receive?
- Who will be on your treatment team, and what will their responsibilities be?
- Will you be placed in a unit specifically designed for adolescents?
- If you are a student, will you be able to continue your schoolwork?
- Will family members be involved in your treatment?
- How long are you expected to stay in the hospital?
- How will the decision to discharge you from the hospital be made?
- Once you are discharged, what follow-up care will be available?

- Psychiatric exam—Performed by a psychiatrist, a medical doctor who specializes in the diagnosis and treatment of mental illnesses and emotional problems. The exam usually involves one to three private sessions with the psychiatrist, who will talk with you, ask questions, and observe your behavior. Often, the psychiatrist will want to talk with your parents also to learn more about your past experiences and medical history as well as your current symptoms.

Snapshots of the Brain

Day six of my hospital stay brought a change of pace. I was taken to a medical hospital across town for a computed tomography (CT) scan. This imaging test uses special x-ray equipment that rotates around part of your body to produce images from many different angles. A powerful computer then combines these images to create a cross-sectional picture of tissues and organs there. In my case, the doctor wanted to see if there were other things besides depression, such as lesions or tumors, going on inside my brain that could explain my symptoms.

When I first arrived at the other hospital, an IV was inserted into my hand. Then I was taken to the CT scan room, where I caught my first glimpse of the bulky scanner, which looked like something out of a science fiction movie. It was a large machine with a hole in the center, something like a high-tech doughnut. I was asked to lie down on a table with my head positioned against a groove that helped hold it still. The nurse explained that I would be able to communicate via a two-way speaker inside the machine, and she put goggles over my eyes. Then the table was rolled into the hole in the scanner. I could hear the clicking and whirring of equipment turning around my head. For a minute, I could feel my surroundings closing in, but the scan was over quickly.

One day, doctors might be able to use newer, more sophisticated brain imaging techniques to look for signs of depression itself. For now, though, brain imaging is used when a doctor wants to rule out other conditions. For example, depending on the specific symptoms you're having, the doctor might want to rule out a brain tumor or nervous system disorder such as multiple sclerosis. Once other possible causes for your symptoms have been excluded, the doctor can be more confident that depression is the true cause.

- Medical exam—Performed by a doctor or other medical professional. The goal is to identify other medical conditions that could be causing or contributing to your symptoms. In addition to performing a physical exam, the doctor may sometimes order specific lab tests.
- Psychological evaluation—Performed by a psychologist, another type of mental health professional who provides

assessment and treatment for mental and emotional disorders. The evaluation typically includes tests that assess your intelligence and personality.

Frankly, going through all this testing can be a pain. After a few days, I got very tired of people poking around inside my mind. It serves a useful purpose, though, because it helps your treatment providers understand your problems and identify likely causes. Armed with this information, they can design a treatment plan that's custom-tailored to your individual needs.

I got very tired of people poking around inside my mind.

Other Treatment Settings

A hospital is just one of several treatment settings. There is a range of other possibilities as your symptoms become less urgent and severe. When you first get out of the hospital, you may still need fairly intensive treatment with psychotherapy, medications, or both. Group therapy and support groups also may be part of the mix. (These treatment approaches are discussed in more detail in Chapter 5.) As you get better, you will gradually need fewer and less intensive services.

Of course, most people with depression never require hospitalization at all. If you fall into this group, less intensive services may be all you ever need. Below are some of the treatment settings that may be used in place of or as a follow-up to hospital care:

- Residential treatment center—A facility where you live in a dorm-like setting with a group of people your age. The treatment there is less specialized and intensive than in a hospital, but your stay may last for weeks or months. In contrast, a hospital stay for depression typically lasts no more than several days.

"My parents think inpatient treatment in a hospital will help me, but I don't agree. What are my legal rights?"

For help answering this question, I consulted Robert Dinerstein, a professor of law and director of the Disability Rights Law Clinic at American University's Washington College of Law in Washington, D.C. It turns out that the answer depends both on your age and where you live. If you are 18 or older, you can't be placed in a psychiatric hospital involuntarily except under very specific circumstances. The laws defining these circumstances vary from state to state. However, most states allow a doctor to order involuntary hospitalization for a short evaluation period, usually three days. For such orders, the doctor must certify that you are an imminent danger to yourself or others. Typically, the doctor is a psychiatrist (some states require two psychiatrists).

After that, if the evaluation team believes a longer hospital stay is needed but you don't agree, a court hearing is required before you can be compelled to stay in the hospital. At the hearing, the state must show that strict criteria have been met. One situation in which you can be involuntarily kept in a psychiatric hospital is when you pose a danger to yourself or others. In some states, you also can be involuntarily hospitalized if you are gravely disabled by a mental disorder, to the point where you can't make a rational decision for yourself. Of course, whether or not you meet these standards, you always have the option of *voluntarily* signing yourself into the hospital if you think that's the right step for you.

If you are under 18, the answer is a bit more complicated. In general, minors aren't afforded the same legal rights as adults. Parents may be able to sign a minor into a psychiatric hospital without the minor's consent, because the court assumes that adults are better able to make this type of decision. There are still some restrictions—even a minor can't be forced to enter a psychiatric hospital without a legitimate reason. The hospital admission must be reviewed by a neutral fact-finder, who has the authority to reject the admission if it is deemed inappropriate. Rather than a judge or hearing officer, though, this fact-finder may be another mental health professional.

That's the usual scenario for minors who are treated as children under the law. When it comes to psychiatric hospitalization, however, several states have passed laws that extend adult-like legal protections to some adolescents under age 18. But even if you are legally able to second-guess your parents' decision, that doesn't necessarily mean you should. In fact, in the vast majority of cases, you probably shouldn't.

Ask yourself whether your parents generally have made good decisions for you in the past. If so, it's likely they are acting in your best interest now, too. Also, give careful thought to the recommendation of your psychiatrist, who has substantial training and experience in making these kinds of decisions. Keep in mind that depression could be coloring your judgment, and listen to the advice of those you trust. I'm very grateful that's the path I chose 11 years ago, because without immediate, intensive treatment, my own story might have had a much different ending.

- Crisis residential treatment—Temporary, 24-hour mental health care in a nonhospital setting during a crisis; for example, if you have a violent blowup. The goal is to give an explosive situation time to cool off. Before going home, you'll also have a chance to plan for the next step in your treatment.
- Partial hospitalization—A treatment option where you spend at least four hours a day on therapy and other treatment-related services, but go home at night. A wide range of services may be provided, such as individual or group therapy, special education, job training, and therapeutic recreational activities.
- Outpatient treatment—A treatment option where you live at home and go to school as usual, but occasionally see a doctor or therapist. The frequency of visits can range from a few times a week to once a month or less, depending on how you're doing. This is the most common mode of mental health care.

My hope for you is that you will never need to see the inside of a psychiatric hospital. But if your depression ever does become so severe that nothing else seems to help or you start thinking about suicide, my hope is that you'll receive the round-the-clock care you need. At the lowest point in my life, less drastic measures simply weren't enough to break through the thick wall of despair and hopelessness that I had constructed. By the time I left the hospital, though, cracks had started to appear in the wall. I still had a big job ahead of me, but I had taken a critical first step toward feeling better.

Less drastic measures simply weren't enough to break through the thick wall of despair and hopelessness that I had constructed.

Chapter Five

Back Among the Living: Medicine and Therapy

My Story

I stuck my arm out the car window and felt the hot wind blowing on my skin. My hand opened and closed under the force of the wind as we drove down the interstate. After eight days in a psychiatric hospital, it was a relief to finally be sitting in the car next to my mom, speeding toward home.

By the time we got there, the midsummer sun was beating down intensely. My dad was home, and he came outside to help unload the car. He gave me a hug, and I knew then he was very thankful I had survived my darkest time, even though it was still hard for him to put those feelings into words.

My brother was at work. This was the first summer that he was old enough to have a real job, and he was working at the school on the maintenance crew. Andy liked this kind of work because it was physical labor. Even after a long day in the heat, he would still have enough energy left to lift weights for a couple of hours. The rest of his time was spent on an active social life as well as his 4-H livestock projects. I think Andy stayed so busy partly because he didn't know how to handle my situation.

Interacting with me was more trouble than it was worth to him at the time.

Inside the house, all I wanted to do was lie down on the couch, watch a movie, and savor my freedom from the hospital's strict time limits and rules. After a small dinner, that's exactly what I did. Before long, I drifted off into a dreamless sleep that was blessedly free of nightmares and awakenings.

Rx: Meds and Therapy

I knew I had a long, hard road ahead of me. My body was still adjusting to the medicine I had started in the hospital, and I knew there were no guarantees it would work. Dr. M. had explained to me that each person's brain chemistry is unique, so the same medication that works wonders for one person might not do a thing for someone else. I wanted the medication to work in minutes, but Dr. M. said it could be weeks before I felt the full benefits. In the meantime, my mom and I should watch for side effects and any changes in my mental state.

It's easier to become invested in any relationship when you know it has the potential to last.

I resumed my therapy sessions with Ms. S. the next day. I had talked a lot while in the hospital, but I didn't feel the same connection to the therapist there as I did to Ms. S. Maybe that was because I knew I might be seeing Ms. S. for a while. It's easier to become invested in any relationship when you know it has the potential to last. As it turned out, I wound up seeing Ms. S. for two more years.

At our first post-hospital visit, Ms. S. was intent on making sure I wasn't still having suicidal thoughts. She reiterated the importance of telling someone if the thoughts recurred. I said that wouldn't be a problem. I felt closer to my mom than to anyone else in the world. In my mind, the fact that I *hadn't* confided in her about my earlier suicidal feelings was a huge failure on my part.

When Ms. S. heard this, she told me something I would never forget: "You are not your depression." She pointed out that depression was a disease, not a moral failing. Part of me knew she was right, but another part didn't quite believe it yet. At that point, I was still awash in guilt and self-reproach.

After our appointment, Ms. S. walked me out to the lobby to meet my mom. Along the way, she commented again about the improvement in my appearance since the first time we had met. Her words were reassuring, but I felt completely exhausted after talking for an hour. It's amazing how draining it can be to lay all the contents of your head out on the table for inspection.

On the way home, my mom and I stopped at our favorite Italian restaurant to "celebrate" making it through the appointment. My mom always found something to celebrate in my accomplishments, no matter how insignificant they might seem. We hit the after-dinner lull, so the restaurant was calm and quiet. The food still didn't taste as good as I knew it was, but I managed to eat a little.

Afterward, we stopped by the grocery store. Waiting in the car while my mom went inside, I turned over the key and switched on the radio. Through the windshield, I watched the sun go down as the sky faded into a gray backdrop mottled with deep purple tones. I flipped through radio stations, trying to find a song that would distract me, but nothing good was on. Soon, my thoughts started to drift back to the vivid nightmare I had before going into the hospital—the one about my own funeral. A single hot tear rolled from my eye, followed by another. I was relieved to be back on familiar turf, but I still had a lot of healing left to do.

Naming the Beast

A few days later, during another excursion with my mom, I told her about the beast for the first time. Naming my depression "the beast" made it easier for me to explain what I was going through. I could finally describe what I was feeling more objectively, without judgment or self-blame. *I* wasn't flawed. I was simply a person with an illness, a chemical imbalance—a beast. I have since heard other people name their depression. The names are different, but the common thread seems to be separating themselves from their illness in order to see it more clearly.

I wasn't flawed. I was simply a person with an illness, a chemical imbalance—a beast. I have since heard other people name their depression.

When I got home, I began drawing pictures of the beast. I drew it consuming me, feeding on my positive emotions, growing larger as I shrank. Although the pictures were disturbing to my mom, she was grateful that I was getting the images out of my head. Ultimately, those images would serve as an incredible communication medium between me and my family, friends, and mental health care providers.

Time passed, and my first visit with Dr. M. since the hospital finally rolled around. The medicine I was taking hadn't caused any nasty side effects. On the other hand, my depression hadn't subsided the way I had hoped it would. I was still feeling extremely sad and apathetic. It seemed that the first medication I had tried wasn't the right one for me after all. Dr. M. assured me this was nothing to be concerned about. He already had another medication in mind for me to try next. Privately, though, I was very discouraged. *How can I get better if the medicine won't even work?* I wondered.

Although I had my doubts, I put my trust in Dr. M., and I started taking the new medicine he prescribed. Over the next couple of weeks, as we waited to see how well this one would work, my dad and I started a new project together. Since I've always loved Volkswagen Beetles, we decided to rebuild one. My dad was amazing with cars, and although he still struggled to express his emotions, this was one way he could be present in my life.

We went in 50/50 on buying a beat-up, run-down '71 Super Beetle convertible. Then we towed the shell of the car, minus four fenders, to a garage where we could work on it. Only people like us—people with a true appreciation for the Beetle—could see the beauty hiding behind that worn-out exterior, just waiting for a little love and attention to bring it out.

My dad and I didn't talk much while we worked on stripping the Beetle of its old seals, gaskets, and upholstery. Sweat rolled off our faces as we worked in the stifling garage. By the end of our first day of work, we knew this was going to be a bigger job than we had anticipated. It didn't matter; I enjoyed watching my dad mess around with the engine. I was constantly learning from him, even when he didn't say a lot. The Beetle was a great distraction from the beast.

Life in the Super-Slow Lane

Before I knew it, summer was almost over—only three weeks left until school started again. I was nervous about seeing my classmates. Everyone else's summer stories would be full of parties, young love, vacations, and sports. Mine would be full of sadness, dark thoughts, hospitalization, and medicine. I had been going to school with many of my classmates since third grade, but they felt like strangers to me. I knew everyone must have heard what happened to me over the summer. How would they treat me? Would I have to answer their questions? Or would they be too afraid to ask?

My life remained stuck in slow motion. Keeping up with everyone else seemed like an impossible task. And I still didn't feel as if I could face being in a crowded building. How was I supposed to handle going to high school?

Despite the medication and therapy sessions twice a week with Ms. S., I felt like I wasn't making any real progress. I was still locked in my sad state of mind, and I hadn't yet found the key that would release me. At my next appointment with Dr. M., he decided this medication wasn't working either. He prescribed his third-choice medicine; I tried to see it as another chance at hope, but discouragement was getting the better of me.

That night at home, I broke down. I was talking to my mom at the kitchen table when a wave of despair hit me like a sudden allergic reaction. I began crying, and I felt so weak that I slid to the floor. My mom sat on the kitchen floor and held me while I sobbed violently. I was starting to lose faith that anything could ever help.

Then the doorbell rang, and our dog launched into his usual barking frenzy. My mom answered the door. It was Uncle Jay, my aunt's ex-husband, dropping off a chair. He had known me since I was a baby, but he hadn't been around as often since he and my mom's sister divorced. He could feel the emotionally charged energy in the air as soon as the door opened, and he hesitated a moment before coming inside. My mom wasn't one to hide a display of strong emotion, though. In her mind, now was the best possible time to see another loved one, so she ushered him into the house.

Uncle Jay entered the kitchen just as I was getting up off the floor. I went over to hug him, and he gave me a firm embrace back. After I had regained some composure, he stayed for a while talking with us. It was good having him there, another person sending caring thoughts my way. Looking back, it's obvious how much I benefited from the loving support of my extended family and friends, even though I was in no condition to fully appreciate this fact at the time.

Looking back, it's obvious how much I benefited from the loving support of my extended family and friends, even though I was in no condition to fully appreciate this fact at the time.

Healing as a Family

Throughout this period, I was continuing my therapy sessions with Ms. S. The sessions were surprisingly hard work, but I did feel better afterward. It was a relief to share my thoughts with a neutral party. My next appointment was going to be different, though, because my brother, Andy, would be there. My mom and dad had attended some earlier therapy sessions, and that hadn't seemed like anything out of the ordinary. But the idea of my brother taking part in a session was a little mind-boggling.

When my mom first informed Andy that he was coming to my next therapy appointment, he flat-out refused. I believe his exact words were, "I'm not the crazy one." Then my mom told him that he didn't have a choice. "When have I ever made you do something that wasn't important?" she asked. "You're going because Cait needs you. We're all experiencing her depression, because we're a family." Deep down, my brother trusted my mom's motivation, so he grudgingly agreed. "Fine, I'll go," he said unenthusiastically. "But I won't talk."

When the appointment finally arrived, Andy talked for the whole hour. Afterward, he never mentioned the session, but I think it helped him to have a chance to vent about our home dynamic and his relationship with me. During my crisis, my brother didn't get much attention, and he often felt left out. The session offered him a chance to have his concerns heard by an objective ear.

In other therapy sessions, I was working with Ms. S. to develop the coping skills I would need when I returned to school. I was trying hard to believe that I could cope, but my brain still felt like it was running backward. I became panicky whenever I thought about doing schoolwork, talking about my summer, or walking in the noisy hallways. On top of that, I was afraid I might start crying uncontrollably, and the embarrassment would be more than I could take.

Paintbrush Therapy

Then about a week before school started, I received a phone call out of the blue from the biology teacher, Ms. Moons. She had heard through the grapevine that I had painted murals before, and she wanted to know if I would be interested in painting a mural in the biology room. Ms. Moons thought her classroom was too plain. It didn't match the vibrancy of her love for biology.

My first reaction was pure joy. Her request struck a nerve—the creative nerve that had never been totally numbed by depression. For a moment, the artist in me transcended the disease and reminded me of what it was like to actually feel joyous again. Ms. Moons was totally unaware of my situation. When she placed that call, she didn't realize that her project would serve as a lifeline at a time when my mind was still reeling from despair, anxiety, and self-doubt.

Ms. Moons came by our house the next day to see the murals on my bedroom walls. I explained to her that these murals were just the latest versions, and that five other layers of painting lay underneath. She looked around the room with an expression of awe. Then Ms. Moons turned to me and said that, without a doubt, she wanted me to transform her classroom into a jungle. She would provide all the materials and get the necessary approvals from the school administration. I wholeheartedly agreed to her proposal.

Afterward, Ms. Moons sat at the kitchen table with my mom and me. For the next hour, she heard us pour out everything that had happened in my life over the summer. We opened our hearts to her, and she reacted with compassion. My mom thanked Ms. Moons for giving me this opportunity. She knew that having creative freedom and a large space in which to work would do wonders for my spirit.

The next day, I met Ms. Moons in her classroom with a written list of all the supplies I would need. She went to get them while I began penciling animal shapes on the cinder block walls. I walked around the room and across lab tables in the new pinstriped painting bibs my dad had bought for me. My pencil seemed to have a life of its own as it sketched life-sized images of jungle animals and plants on all four walls of the room.

It took five days to complete the metamorphosis of the classroom. For the first time in months, I felt as if I had some worth as a human being. Students would walk into the classroom, and their jaws would drop in amazement over the transformation. It seemed everyone was impressed that a fourteen-year-old had accomplished so much in less than a week. Most of them never knew that I felt as if I was also fighting for my life inside my own mind. It was hard to fully absorb the praise, but the confused feeling it aroused was a welcome change of pace.

For the first time in months, I felt as if I had some worth as a human being.

Yet despite completing this impressive creative feat, I still felt fragile as glass in many ways. My fears about rejoining the student population began to return in full force. It was Friday, and classes started on Monday. Suddenly, I was at the bottom of the pecking order again. I was a freshman.

The Big Picture

By summer's end, I was finally starting to feel the positive effects of my treatment. The two main treatment options for depression are psychotherapy (the formal name for "talk therapy") and medication. I wound up on a combination of both. In research, each option has been shown to be helpful, and the one-two punch delivered by both together may be even more powerful than either alone.

For example, take a recent study of 439 depressed adolescents that appeared in *JAMA*, the journal of the American Medical Association. This study looked at the combination of a medication and a popular form of psychotherapy called cognitive-behavioral therapy (CBT). The researchers found that 71% of those in the study improved on the combination treatment. That's better than the percentage who responded to either treatment by itself (61% for medication alone and 43% for CBT alone). It's also far better than the percentage (35%) who responded to a placebo, a sugar pill that looks like the real thing but doesn't contain any active ingredient. Placebos are used in research to see how much physiological effect a treatment has over and above the psychological effect of just believing that it will help.

Whenever I read about results like these, I'm encouraged. But I'm also reminded that the first type of medication or therapy tried isn't always going to work. In the study, over a quarter of the teens weren't helped by this particular combination of treatments. For me, it also took a few tries to find the right medication. At times, I was tempted to give up, but I just told myself to have faith. It took patience, but eventually my doctor and I found the right medication for me.

Treatment With Medication

Depression is rooted in a chemical imbalance within the brain, so it makes sense that the problem might respond to a chemical treatment. Antidepressants are drugs used to prevent or relieve depression. As I discovered, there are many different antidepressants available. For adults with depression, these drugs have proved to be generally safe and effective. Less research has been done in teenagers. Overall, though, studies and experience show that antidepressants can be quite helpful for teens as well.

Selective Serotonin Reuptake Inhibitors

The best-studied antidepressants in teens are selective serotonin reuptake inhibitors, or SSRIs. When SSRIs first appeared in the 1980s, they were welcomed as a big advance. These drugs were thought to be as effective as tricyclic antidepressants, an older type of depression medicine. However, SSRIs didn't cause as many troublesome side effects. SSRIs include citalopram (Celexa), escitalopram (Lexapro), fluoxetine (Prozac), fluvoxamine (Luvox), paroxetine (Paxil), and sertraline (Zoloft). Today, when a doctor writes a prescription for depression, an SSRI is usually the first medication that's tried.

Serotonin is a chemical messenger in the brain, and low levels of serotonin are thought to play a key role in depression. As their name implies, SSRIs work by inhibiting the reuptake of serotonin. In plain English, this means they interfere with the absorption of the chemical back into the brain cells that first released it. The result is that more serotonin is available for use by the brain. SSRIs also seem to change the number and sensitivity of the brain's serotonin receptors.

Newer Antidepressants

Over the last couple of decades, SSRIs have become the gold standard in depression medication, but they're no longer the new kids on the block. Since the late 1990s, several newer antidepressants have been introduced. Some newer antidepressants—including bupropion (Wellbutrin) and mirtazapine (Remeron)—are chemically unrelated to SSRIs. Others—including venlafaxine (Effexor) and duloxetine (Cymbalta)—affect serotonin the same way SSRIs do, plus they also slow the reuptake of another brain chemical called norepinephrine. Like SSRIs, the newer antidepressants are helpful for many people. However, they haven't been as extensively studied in adolescents, so they aren't as widely prescribed.

Other Antidepressants

SSRIs and newer antidepressants are widely used, and the older tricyclic antidepressants are still sometimes prescribed as well. However, a fourth type of antidepressant, called monoamine oxidase inhibitors (MAOIs), is rarely prescribed for teenagers. Although MAOIs may help some adults who don't respond to other antidepressants, people taking them have to adhere to a strictly limited diet, which generally makes them unsuitable for young people.

What to Expect From Medication

Depression isn't like strep throat. You can't just take a pill for a few days and expect to be well. Instead, getting better from depression requires a long-term commitment to yourself. If you

Antidepressants

Type of antidepressant	*Generic name*	*Usual brand name*
Selective serotonin reuptake inhibitors (SSRIs)	Citalopram	Celexa
	Escitalopram	Lexapro
	Fluoxetine	Prozac
	Fluvoxamine	Luvox
	Paroxetine	Paxil
	Sertraline	Zoloft
Newer antidepressants	Bupropion	Wellbutrin
	Duloxetine	Cymbalta
	Mirtazapine	Remeron
	Venlafaxine	Effexor
Tricyclic antidepressants (TCAs)	Amitriptyline	Elavil
	Clomipramine	Anafranil
	Desipramine	Norpramin
	Doxepin	Sinequan
	Imipramine	Tofranil
	Maprotiline	Ludiomil
	Nortriptyline	Pamelor
	Protriptyline	Vivactil
	Trimipramine	Surmontil

have moderate to severe symptoms the way I did, medication can help on its own, or if you are receiving psychotherapy, medication can help you improve enough to focus on the therapy process. Even if your symptoms are milder, medication may be prescribed if you've tried psychotherapy but found it didn't provide enough relief by itself. In addition, medication is often helpful if you're prone to long-lasting or recurring episodes of depression.

Don't expect overnight results. It may take four to six weeks to feel the full effects of an antidepressant. If you still aren't feeling better after that time, your doctor may try increasing your dose, switching to another drug, or

Don't expect overnight results. It may take four to six weeks to feel the full effects of an antidepressant.

adding a second medicine. There's no way to know in advance which drug will work for which person, so it may take some trial and error to find the best medication for you.

Once an effective medication has been found, it's usually continued for six months to a year and sometimes longer. This helps prevent the depression from returning. If you stop taking an antidepressant too soon or too abruptly, the depression may return, so be sure to follow your doctor's instructions.

All medications have the potential to cause unintended effects, known as side effects. Antidepressants are no exception. SSRIs sometimes cause headaches, nausea, and problems with sexual functioning. Newer antidepressants can cause similar problems. In addition, some people who take antidepressants develop anxiety, panic attacks, trouble sleeping, irritability, hostility, impulsiveness, agitation, or extreme restlessness. It's thought that some people who develop these symptoms soon after starting an antidepressant may be at increased risk for suicidal thoughts. If you notice these symptoms in yourself, be sure to *let your doctor know right away.*

The Facts About Supplements

Antidepressants have to be powerful in order to work, but that potency means they also carry some risks. You might wonder whether dietary supplements are a safer alternative. Unfortunately, it's not that simple. Because supplements don't have to go through the same rigorous approval process as drugs, the manufacturers aren't required to show that they're effective. Also, just like drugs, supplements can cause unintended effects.

One of the most popular supplements for treating depression is an herb called St. John's wort *(Hypericum perforatum),* which is a prescription medication in Europe. In the United States, where it's sold without a prescription, it's one of the top-selling herbal

The Not-So-Shocking Truth About "Shock Therapy"

Medication and psychotherapy are the most common treatments for depression. However, electroconvulsive therapy (ECT) is another option that's occasionally used to treat severe symptoms. This treatment is reserved for the most severe cases, where at least two medications have been tried without success or the symptoms are so urgent that there isn't time to wait for medication to work.

In ECT, a carefully controlled electrical current is delivered to the brain, where it produces a brief seizure. This is thought to alter some of the electrical and chemical processes involved in brain functioning. Studies have shown that ECT can indeed be quite helpful for many people with severe depression. Unfortunately, ECT is sometimes referred to as "shock therapy," a misnomer that has helped give the therapy an undeserved bad rap in the public mind. Although I never actually had ECT, Dr. M. mentioned it as a possibility at one point, and it was hard for me to get the image of being electrocuted out of my mind.

In truth, the procedure isn't nearly as scary as its nickname makes it sound. A person receiving ECT is first given medication that keeps him or her from feeling pain and prevents the body from convulsing. The seizure is contained within the brain, and it only lasts for about a minute. A few minutes later, the person awakens, just as someone would after minor surgery.

ECT usually consists of 6 to 12 such treatments, which are typically given three times a week. The effects appear gradually over the course of treatment, although they may be felt sooner than with medication and/or psychotherapy. The most common immediate side effects of ECT are headaches, muscle soreness, nausea, and confusion. Such effects generally clear up quickly. As the treatments go on, some people also develop problems with memory. While most of these problems clear up within days to months after the last ECT treatment, they occasionally last longer. On the flip side, some people say their memory is actually better after ECT, because their mind is no longer operating in a fog of depression.

products. St. John's wort may help very mild depressive symptoms. But a large, carefully designed study funded by the National Institutes of Health found that it was no more effective than a placebo for treating moderate depression. Also, St. John's wort can cause side effects, including dry mouth, dizziness, diarrhea, nausea, fatigue, and increased sensitivity to sunlight. Plus, St. John's wort may interact with several medications, including birth control pills, decreasing their effectiveness. It's also possible that St. John's wort may interact harmfully with certain antidepressants, including SSRIs.

If you're thinking about trying a supplement, talk to your doctor first. Your doctor can help you decide whether it's a safe and sensible idea for you. If you do take a supplement, think of it as something you use *along with* your medication and therapy, not *instead of* them. There's no evidence that supplements alone can take the place of standard medical treatments for depression.

If you're thinking about trying a supplement, talk to your doctor first.

Treatment With Psychotherapy

Depression has a major effect on the way a person thinks, acts, and relates to other people. Problems in these areas, in turn, can make the depression worse. While medication targets the biological roots of depression, psychotherapy targets the psychological, behavioral, and social aspects.

Cognitive-Behavioral Therapy

CBT is the best-studied form of psychotherapy for treating depression in young people. The goal of this type of therapy is to change habitual patterns of thinking and acting that may be contributing to a person's problems. The cognitive part involves learning to identify unrealistically negative thoughts and re-

Guy's-Eye View

Even after Sanjay was diagnosed with depression at age 16, he was hesitant to take his medication. Sanjay's mother worked in the health care field, so she was comfortable in the medical world. But whenever possible, she preferred to rely on the holistic, natural approach to healing that she had grown up with in India. Sanjay, too, was skeptical. He says, "I would start taking a medication, but then I'd go off it without telling anyone, so I never saw any long-term positive results."

"It wasn't until the spring of my sophomore year in college that I realized medication really did help," Sanjay says. Once he started taking his medication consistently, his symptoms receded, his grades improved, and the bouts of disabling depression stopped recurring so frequently.

Before that, Sanjay had fallen into a common trap. "I would go off my meds as soon as I started feeling happy and well, only to have the depression return shortly thereafter," he says. Another time, Sanjay stopped taking his medication right before his freshman year of college because he was afraid of what the other students might think. He wound up missing the first three semesters of college as he fought his way out of that depression. Eventually, Sanjay wised up. "I realized this was a sign that long-term stability wasn't going to be possible for me without medication." He has been taking his medication consistently ever since.

Sanjay no longer worries about hiding his depression from his roommates, who turned out not to be bothered by it after all. In fact, he says, "I keep my pillbox in a prominent place on my desk, right next to where I pick up my glasses in the morning. It's a good reminder to take my pills every day."

place them with more realistically positive ones. The behavioral part involves changing self-defeating behaviors as well as learning more effective coping skills.

In CBT, a person might learn to:

- Think more optimistically
- Monitor mood changes
- Plan pleasant activities

- Set and achieve goals
- Relax and manage stress

Interpersonal Therapy

Interpersonal therapy (IPT) is another form of psychotherapy that has proved to be effective against depression. The idea behind IPT is simple: Whatever the cause of depression, its symptoms are often set off by a relationship problem. This problem typically involves a change in social role, the lack of social skills, a dispute with another person, or grief over a personal loss. IPT helps a person identify the problem that triggered a bout of depression. Then the person learns the necessary social and communication skills to resolve that problem successfully.

IPT helps a person identify the problem that triggered a bout of depression.

In IPT, a person might learn to:

- Resolve family conflicts
- Adjust to a new step-family
- Form healthy friendships
- Deal with peer pressure
- Establish an independent identity

Family Therapy

Often, you'll work one-on-one with your therapist. At times, though, it makes sense to include other people. Family therapy brings several members of a family together for therapy sessions. Speaking for myself, I think it was very beneficial having my parents and brother take part. It helped me open lines of communication with my dad, and it gave my brother a place to vent his frustration over all the attention I was receiving. As my mom said, the whole family was experiencing my depression. Family therapy gave us all a chance to express our feelings, practice our communication skills, and learn new strategies for facing this challenge.

Group Therapy

Group therapy is another option that was quite helpful for me when I was in the hospital. It brings together several patients with similar diagnoses or issues for therapy sessions. In my case, there were three of us who were all about the same age and struggling with suicidal feelings. Under the guidance of our therapist, we listened to each other's stories and shared our heartfelt emotional support. I found it reassuring to know that there were other people my age who accepted me, understood my feelings, and knew what it was like to battle the same dark demons.

I found it reassuring to know that there were other people my age who accepted me, understood my feelings, and knew what it was like to battle the same dark demons.

What to Expect From Psychotherapy

Numerous studies have now demonstrated the value of both CBT and IPT for depression treatment. CBT has been particularly well researched in young people with depression. Its effectiveness has been shown in a wide range of treatment formats, including both individual and group therapy with a varying number of sessions. Several different types of mental health professionals provide psychotherapy, including psychologists, psychiatrists, clinical social workers, mental health counselors, psychiatric nurses, and marriage and family therapists.

Psychotherapy isn't something that just happens to you, though. It's something you help create for yourself, so it requires your active participation. Even though you're just sitting and talking, therapy can be surprisingly hard work, but it's well worth the effort. The more you put into the experience, the more you

Psychotherapy isn't something that just happens to you, though. It's something you help create for yourself, so it requires your active participation.

get back in terms of new emotional, behavioral, and social skills.

Psychotherapy is sometimes used alone for milder depression. It's often combined with medication when the depression is moderate to severe. In my experience, you'll get more out of your therapy sessions if you approach them with a spirit of trust and cooperation. Also, the more honest you can be, the better—even if it means opening up about thoughts, feelings, and experiences that are painful to talk about. For me, it wasn't easy to own up to my suicidal thoughts. I was deeply ashamed—I thought they were a sign that I was damaged and worthless. As hard as it was, though, sharing those thoughts was a first step toward reclaiming my life.

In studies of CBT, good results generally have been achieved in anywhere from 5 to 16 sessions. But the exact number of sessions *you* will need depends on several factors, including how severe your symptoms are and whether you have any coexisting conditions. It's possible you might need to continue therapy longer, the way I did. At first, the sessions may be scheduled weekly or more often. As you start feeling better, though, the sessions might be spaced farther apart.

If you expect instant results, you're likely to be disappointed. As with medication, psychotherapy takes time to work. At some point in the first few sessions, you and your therapist will probably create a list of goals. If you feel like you haven't made progress toward those goals after several sessions, don't be afraid to bring this up to your therapist. It's possible you've made more progress than you realize. Of course, it's also possible you might benefit from a new approach. Try to remain flexible as you and your therapist work together to find the best approach for you.

"Why do I feel more depressed in winter, and what can I do about it?"

Some people have a form of depression called seasonal affective disorder (SAD), in which the symptoms come and go around the same time each year. Typically, the symptoms begin in the fall or winter and subside in the spring. While many people may have a mild case of the winter doldrums, those with SAD sink into a full-blown episode of major depression. Such episodes are thought to be linked to the shorter days and reduced exposure to sunlight in the winter.

Why would lack of sunlight make someone feel depressed? Scientists still aren't sure about the reason. However, one theory points to a hormone called melatonin. This hormone regulates the body's internal clock, which controls the timing of daily fluctuations in sleep, body temperature, and hormone secretion. Melatonin production goes up during periods of darkness, so winter's short, gloomy days may lead to an abundance of the hormone. In some people, this might trigger depression symptoms. Another theory suggests that light may alter the activity of serotonin or other brain chemicals that are involved in depression.

If lack of light is the problem, then it stands to reason that exposing people to more light might be part of the solution. That's the rationale for light therapy, a treatment sometimes prescribed for SAD. Light therapy involves daily exposure to a very bright light from an artificial source. Typically, this means sitting in front of a special light box that contains extra-bright fluorescent bulbs or tubes covered by a plastic screen. A person might gradually work up to spending 30 to 60 minutes a day in front of the box at a designated time, usually in the morning.

In adults with SAD, researchers have gotten good results using light therapy. However, it isn't known whether the treatment works equally well in teenagers. Light therapy can cause side effects, including eyestrain, headache, and irritability. Also, it may not be appropriate for everyone, including those who have light-sensitive skin or an eye condition that makes them especially prone to eye damage. Because of these risks, light therapy should only be used under the guidance of a professional. Talk to your doctor or therapist if you're wondering whether light therapy might be right for you. In some cases, extra light may brighten up your mood.

Joining a Support Group

Support groups are different from group therapy. The meetings aren't necessarily guided by a professional, and the members aren't working toward formal treatment goals. Instead, support groups are more like a club where all the members share a common problem. Some groups are geared specifically to teenagers or college students with depression and other mental health concerns.

Support groups can be a great place to share emotional comfort and practical advice with other people who know what it's really like to have depression. The other members often can point you toward helpful resources in your community. Such groups are also a good place to find inspiration, since there's nothing more encouraging than meeting someone who has fought the same battle and won.

Your therapist or psychiatrist may be able to suggest a support group in your area. In addition, the Depression and Bipolar Support Alliance (800-826-3632, www.dbsalliance.org) has chapters around the country that offer more than 1,000 support groups. Along with meetings, some chapters also offer educational classes, newsletters, lending libraries, and special events.

Online support groups are another possibility. They're available 24/7, no matter where you live. If you're the type of person who spends half your free time surfing the Web or sending text messages, this method of getting and giving support may feel like second nature. Just keep in mind the same safe surfing precautions you would use when meeting anyone on the Web. Never give out personal information, such as your phone number and home address, because you can't be certain who's on the other end of a virtual conversation. Also, for most

Online support groups are another possibility.

people, online interactions will never match the warmth of a face-to-face friendship. But they can be a useful addition to the other sources of support and comfort in your life.

Getting the Help You Need

When you're mentally exhausted and emotionally drained, you may not have the energy or drive to reach out for help. Ask someone you trust to give you a hand. My mom was my motivator. For you, it might be another relative, your best friend, or a doctor, teacher, school counselor, sports coach, or religious adviser.

During those first few appointments, just knowing that my mom was sitting in the waiting room was a source of strength for me. If you think it would help, you can ask a family member or friend to accompany you to your first appointment, too. They don't necessarily have to participate. Just having someone there who cares may provide the extra motivational boost you need.

Getting treatment isn't a passive process. You play an active role, whether it's by making sure you take your medicine or by giving your best effort to therapy. Don't worry if it feels like you're just barely dragging yourself through at first. That's to be expected—it's the depression at work. After a few weeks, it starts to feel a little easier. As time goes on and the treatment takes a more secure hold, you'll eventually be able to give it your all.

There were so many times when I was tempted to wonder whether treatment was pointless. It's a seductive message when you're already tired and despairing. Ultimately, though, I chose to listen to my loved ones and the professionals who were urging me to give treatment a chance. It was one of the smartest choices I've ever made in my life.

Chapter Six

Bumps in the Road: Coping in Everyday Life

My Story

The night before school started, I lay awake staring at the artwork covering my bedroom walls. My brother was already totally focused on the upcoming football season, and some of my friends had started training for fall sports, too. I should have been training for volleyball, but not this year. I couldn't imagine juggling both school and sports. School alone was going to be enough of a challenge.

I could hear the television downstairs, which meant my mom couldn't sleep either. She had done all she could to make the transition back to school as painless as possible, but I knew she was deeply apprehensive. After that initial burst of creative energy when I was asked to paint the classroom mural, the dark thoughts and lethargic feelings had begun to creep back. The medicine still wasn't helping as much as it should, and my mind and body remained racked with depression.

Eventually, I dozed off, but morning came much too soon. Anxiety filled my thoughts from the moment I opened by eyes. My clothes for the day were neatly laid out, courtesy of my mom, who didn't want me to have to think about anything other than just making it through the day. After I dressed, she drove me to school, and the closer we got, the more I could feel my stomach tighten into a knot of fear. My nervousness was palpable. "All you have to do today is breathe, nothing else," my mom reassured me. Her expectations of me had clearly been lowered several notches, but she still knew how to say exactly the right thing at the right time.

"All you have to do today is breathe, nothing else."

When we pulled up to the school and I looked at those familiar double doors, I remembered the last time I had walked through them when school was in session. Everything had changed in just a matter of months. I was back in the same place, but I was miles away from the person I had been before.

The 15-Minute Freshman

As soon as I entered the school, I found myself swept up into the river of students flowing through the hall. Every time someone brushed against me, even slightly, my muscles would tighten and my skin would crawl. My breath came faster as the panicky feelings began to rise. Earlier that week, Ms. Moons had offered her classroom as a safe haven, saying I was always welcome there. Remembering her offer, I headed straight for the biology room.

Making my way through the hall, I saw some of my friends standing by their lockers. They were buzzing about their summers, the way I would have been a year ago. Now I couldn't even bear to talk with them. All I could think about was making it to safety. By the time I ducked into the biology room, Ms. Moons could see the panic on my face. She tried to comfort me by telling me about all the compliments my mural had received, but I didn't really hear her. My mind was off someplace else, detached from the reality around me.

The warning bell for first period brought me back with a start. I glanced at my schedule and saw that theology class was up first. Reentering the bustling hallway, I felt like I was stepping into speeding traffic. Then suddenly Liz was by my side, giving me a warm hug. Her face said volumes about how much she had missed me. For the past few months, she had been totally cut off from her closest friend, and I knew that must have been hard for her.

Many of my other classmates hurried by without a word. Were they avoiding me? Or were they just distracted by the excitement of seeing everyone again? News travels fast in a small community, so I was sure everyone must have heard about what happened to me that summer. A few friends did come up and ask how I was doing. I could guess what was going through their minds, because I had wondered the same thing myself: How could I, class clown and life of the party, have ended up so depressed? The fact that I didn't have an answer only made me feel worse.

How could I, class clown and life of the party, have ended up so depressed?

Finally, I reached the door of my first period classroom, and that's when I saw the note. "Phys ed today," it read. Too late, I remembered that theology class and phys ed alternated days. I didn't have my gym clothes with me, because I had completely forgotten about this scheduling anomaly. I felt my face growing hot with embarrassment, and tears welled up in my eyes. *Don't cry—this is no big deal,* I told myself, but it made no difference. The tears were already spurting out uncontrollably. Luckily, the hall was empty by that time, so no one witnessed my outburst. But the walls were closing in, and I had to get out of there.

I ran to the office. When I arrived, the secretary asked what was wrong, but I was too distraught to speak. The longer I stood there crying, the more upset I became. My mom had already informed the school about my illness, so the principal recognized this overreaction as a symptom and called my mom at work. Meanwhile, I sat in the waiting area, acutely aware that my face must be bright red. A couple of people walked past, and I was sure they were staring at me. All I wanted to do was run out of the building and scream to the world that I was emphatically *not ready to be back!*

When the principal hung up the phone, she told me I could go home. I felt weak, weary, and downhearted. It was warm and sunny out, but I felt trapped in my own personal storm cloud. Paranoid thoughts thundered through my brain, and tears once again poured from my eyes. I was deeply disappointed in myself and disenchanted with the world in general. My mom was also concerned and maybe a little surprised. We had both known this day was going to be difficult for me, but we hadn't anticipated the intensity of my reaction. I had only made it 15 minutes into my freshman year.

Indefinite Absence

My mom then called an emergency meeting with the faculty and staff at the school. By the time they met the next day, she already had a plan in mind. She would take a leave of absence from her teaching job at another school so that she could homeschool me. My mom would coordinate with each of my teachers to get the homework and tests for my courses. That way, I wouldn't fall behind my classmates, and as I got better, I could gradually ease back into my regular schedule.

I honestly had no opinion about the plan. All I cared about was staying out of that stressful and overwhelming school environment. My mom went to great lengths to work out all the details with the school, but she handled everything so well that she made this complicated arrangement look easy. It wasn't until later in life that I fully realized the pains she took and sacrifices she made on my behalf.

Next to my mom and me, Liz was probably the person most affected by the plan. She had hoped her best friend would be back into the swing of things and we could pick up where we had left off before the summer. Liz was disappointed, but she understood that depression was an illness, not a choice I was making.

Later that week, I had an appointment with Dr. M. Downspirited, I listened as he explained that he was changing my treatment regimen yet again. This time, he was going to try combining two different medications. I didn't really believe this combination of drugs would work, and I said as much to my mom in the car. If even medicine didn't help, what did that say about me? Was I doomed to feel this way forever? The thought was terrifying. I felt like crawling into a hole and never emerging.

My mom and I stayed in the city a while longer so that I could have a therapy session with Ms. S. that same evening. It was a welcome chance to talk with someone removed from my day-to-day life, and I poured out my heart to Ms. S. I told her what had happened at school and how I felt like I was on a wild goose chase looking for the right medicine. I confessed that I felt like I was burning out my dad, my brother, my extended family, and, most of all, my mom.

I was sure everyone must be getting tired of me because I wasn't getting better. A lot of time had gone by, and I thought the patience of those closest to me must be wearing thin. Looking back, I don't believe that was ever true, but I was convinced of it at the time. After the session, I felt a small sense of relief from releasing pent-up emotions.

I felt a small sense of relief from releasing pent-up emotions.

Mostly, though, I just felt my usual exhaustion from spending an hour probing the darkness that seemed to rule my mind.

Back home that night, I channeled all my frustration into a disturbing pair of drawings. The first depicted a person who was bursting out of the casing of another body. The person inside was pulling apart the outer body's skin, frantically ripping her way through. For me, the drawing represented how I felt when I still had a glimmer of hope that my treatment would work. In the second picture, I drew the same outer body, but now it was sewn shut, trapping the struggling person inside. That's how I felt now—I had given up hope and felt as if my fate was sealed.

As the week went by, my mom set up a schedule for home schooling. I didn't know it then, but having this type of structure in my life was crucial. In the morning, there was time set aside for doing something that gave me a sense of serenity. Most often, I just wanted to sit in our backyard and watch the birds that frequented the feeders and birdbath. I could sit there for hours listening to the language of the birds, watching their behavior and trying to discern their personalities.

Other mornings, I would take a bike ride with my dad or walk with my mom. Exercise was therapeutic, even if I could only keep it up for a short time. Away from the commotion of people, it was easier to stay physically active. In a crowd, I still felt paralyzed by the onslaught of sights and sounds. But on these quiet mornings, I sometimes found the energy for a brief exercise break.

After this morning activity, my mom and I would sit down at the kitchen table and start working on my assignments. My mom often read the material to me because I was still having trouble making sense of written words. Math also seemed like way too much work to figure out. My mom tried valiantly to make the material interesting, but my brain was just too tired to think.

Oddly enough, the only thing I didn't mind studying was Shakespeare. While the material was difficult to process, I found comfort in the beauty of the language. Many of the metaphors made sense to me, and the deep emotion they conveyed struck a chord as well. It was a reminder that I wasn't the only person who had felt things this intensely. After reading Shakespeare, I didn't feel so alone.

A Break in the Clouds

A couple of weeks later, I noticed that getting out of bed in the morning didn't seem like such a monumental struggle anymore. Searching for reasons, it dawned on me that it had been a few weeks since I started the new combination of medications. *Maybe they're actually working,* I thought incredulously. Instantly, I checked my excitement. I would reserve judgment until I saw whether the feeling lasted. I didn't want to be let down again. This time, though, something felt slightly different. I was less intimidated by the start of the day, less fearful about what might lie ahead.

I noticed that getting out of bed in the morning didn't seem like such a monumental struggle anymore.

To me, it seemed like a small change, but to my mom, it was colossal. After months of worry, she was finally seeing a flicker of light at the end of the tunnel. Over the next few days, my mom noticed several signs of improvement that I had missed until she pointed them out. She actually saw me smile once in a while, and she told me that my eyes looked as if the life was slowly returning to them.

I had been so low for so long that I had forgotten how hope and happiness felt. I was astonished to feel those emotions stirring back to life again. But almost immediately, my thoughts turned to the long road ahead. I realized that I was the only one who could travel it. I had many people in my life who would love and support me, but it was ultimately up to me to make the journey to recovery.

Thinking of the future evoked a deep sense of anxiety. There were so many things I didn't think I could ever do again. Depression was holding on hard, disputing any new, positive feelings I might have. As soon as I had a thought that wasn't totally dark and dismal, a conflicting thought would pop into my mind to contradict it. There was still a war going on inside my brain. But for the first time in months, it was a battle of equals. The medicine had made it a fairer fight.

At my next appointment with Ms. S., she saw the improvement as well. I told her that I felt hope might have a place in my life after all, but I still felt incredibly fragile. I worried that I might break at the slightest wrong move, and I would have to go back to the beginning and start the healing process all over again. Then Ms. S. told me something I would never forget: "You are not fragile," she said. "You are vulnerable." That made sense to me. Fragile meant I might be shattered beyond repair. Vulnerable, on the other hand, meant I might be knocked down, but I would still have a chance of getting up again and surviving.

Back to School, Part Two

Two months passed as I slowly but surely continued to improve. I had kept up academically, thanks to my mom's efforts. Finally, during one of my sessions with Ms. S., my mom and I decided that I should try easing back into school, starting with my art and English classes.

The next morning, my mom drove me to school. We sat in the car out front for a few minutes, and she gave me the same advice she had shared a couple of months earlier. "Just breathe," she said—only this time, I felt as if I might actually be able to heed her advice. She reminded me that my English class was starting to study Shakespeare's *Romeo and Juliet*, one of my favorites.

When I got out of the car, all my old fears came flooding back, but they were toned down just enough to make me believe that it was possible to try again. Entering the school, I waited off to one side to let the busyness of the hallway die down. A few people noticed me through the hustle and bustle, but they didn't say anything. When the last bell rang, I walked to my class. Right before opening the door, I took a deep breath. Then I pulled the door open, walked in, and sat down.

To my surprise, it felt good to be back among my classmates. Many of them smiled a greeting, and there was a little ripple of quiet excitement about my return that I hadn't expected. Sitting there listening to the teacher, it felt good to know that I mattered to the people around me. After class ended, I took my time leaving because the noise in the hallway still made my skin crawl a bit. A couple of my friends waited with me to talk, not caring about getting a tardy from their next teacher. When they asked how I was, the only response I could muster was, "Better."

Then they began updating me about what was happening at school as if I had only been gone for two days, not two months. I couldn't have asked for anything more. I didn't want to dwell on my depression at that moment. I was tired of talking about it and even more tired of feeling it.

As my friends dispersed to their next class, I walked down the nearly empty hallway toward the front door. That's when I saw Liz at her locker and ran to embrace her. She gave me a big hug back before heading off to her next class. "Call me anytime," she said. "Come over when you're ready." As I watched her hurrying off, I thought about what a true friend she had been, no strings attached.

Outside, my mom was waiting for me. We got drive-through drinks and cruised around town talking about my day. It had gone better than expected, and we both wanted to keep the positive momentum rolling. Then my mom had a brainstorm: We would get a new pet. She thought caring for another life would be a healthy distraction for me. After some discussion, we decided that a ferret would be fun, so when my second class was over that afternoon, we went ferret shopping. Glynnis, our new ferret, proved to be much more than a distraction. She quickly made friends with our dog and cat and became a full-fledged member of our family.

My Road to Recovery

Meanwhile, life went on around me. My brother's school year was in full swing. He was a football star with lots of friends, including a steady girlfriend, and he was living the life that was expected of a 16-year-old. My friends were busy with dating, sports, and parties, too, while I spent a lot of time by myself thinking, drawing, and writing. At times, I still felt like a fragment that had been broken off from the rest of society.

With each passing day, however, my condition gradually improved. Slowly, I began to spend more time at school and extracurricular activities. Even the noise in the hallway wasn't bothering me as much as before. Bit by bit, I was starting to rediscover hope, and I was determined to hold onto it.

Then a few weeks later, I had another downturn. Fortunately, my mom had been keeping a detailed log of my behavior, and she noticed a pattern. Once a month, right before I was due to start my menstrual period, I would take a big step backward.

Dr. M. thought premenstrual hormones might be aggravating my symptoms, so he prescribed birth control pills to stabilize my hormonal swings. I hated the idea of taking another medicine, but Dr. M. said this would only be temporary until I was on firmer footing, and I was willing to try anything that might help.

By six months into the school year, I felt as if I had finally gotten the upper hand on my illness. I was back in school full time, and my mom had returned to her job. Many days, I would still drift off into introspection. I would remember how I felt while being consumed by the beast not that long ago. And I would marvel at my progress, even when I needed to retreat from the world temporarily. I didn't see retreat as a setback anymore. Now I saw it as keeping my balance.

Besides getting professional treatment, I took steps to help myself. I looked for activities that fed my soul and threw myself into them with profound intensity. At school, I spent more and more time in the art room. Artwork was gushing from me like blood from a deep wound. The art teacher, who would be my teacher throughout the rest of high school, fostered this creative energy and offered me a safe place for expressing my feelings.

I was becoming more social again, too. I stayed over at Liz's house, went to school events, and even attended some parties. I still tried to avoid crowded places, and to this day, I have trouble coping with crowds. My illness left some scars that never completely healed. But for the most part, I felt as if I had reclaimed my life and rejoined the rest of society.

For me, the road to recovery was filled with twists, turns, and potholes. Traveling this road, I had two major fears. Ironically, one was the fear of reaching my destination. Once I was well, people would expect me to handle life the way a "healthy" person does. Sometimes, I would think that if I stayed sick and depressed, no one would expect anything of me. But eventually, I had a revelation: I would rather deal with whatever came my way than remain a prisoner of this miserable illness.

I would rather deal with whatever came my way than remain a prisoner of this miserable illness.

My second and bigger fear was that I would overcome depression only to have it return again. I knew this was always a possibility. But I held onto the idea that now I would know how to recognize the signs and take action early. I would be able to see the darkness coming before it totally engulfed me.

The Big Picture

This last fear wasn't totally unfounded. Relapse and recurrence are big issues for anyone trying to cope with depression and move on with life. Relapse refers to symptoms that reappear after going away for a short time. Recurrence refers to a whole new episode of an illness after a lengthy period of feeling back to normal. Both are very real concerns.

Over the course of a lifetime, people who don't seek treatment average five to seven episodes of major depression, and the episodes tend to grow worse each time. But by getting treatment, you may interrupt the downward spiral into frequent recurrences. And even if depression does occur again, you'll be better prepared to deal with it.

For me, the ups and downs in my progress were hard to take, and at times they made me feel like all my efforts were pointless. Yet for every step backward, I was actually taking two or three forward. Even though my progress was maddeningly slow at times, I eventually got back to my old self again.

More Than PMS

Up to 40% of menstruating women have premenstrual syndrome (PMS). Common symptoms include tender breasts, abdominal bloating, food cravings, tiredness, mild mood swings, irritability, and a blue mood in the days before a woman's menstrual period begins. Some of the symptoms are similar to those of major depression, but milder and shorter-lived. While the precise cause is still unknown, PMS is thought to be linked in part to monthly changes in hormone levels.

For most women with PMS, the symptoms are uncomfortable or unpleasant, but not to the point where they seriously interfere with daily life. For some women like me, though, the symptoms are more severe and disabling. Premenstrual dysphoric disorder (PMDD) is the fancy name for this condition. PMDD can occur in women with or without depression, but it's more than just a worsening of ongoing symptoms. Instead, there's a cyclic pattern in which certain symptoms arise right before a woman's menstrual period. These symptoms begin to subside within a few days after her period starts, and they disappear in the week after her period ends.

PMDD always involves some type of emotional upheaval, such as intense depression, anxiety, anger, or mood swings. Other possible symptoms include loss of interest in usual activities, trouble concentrating, lack of energy, changes in appetite, sleep problems, a subjective sense of being overwhelmed or out of control, and physical signs such as breast tenderness, headaches, joint or muscle pain, bloating, and weight gain. Because some of these symptoms are so similar to those of depression, doctors think serotonin may play a role in PMDD, too.

Along the way, depression touched virtually every aspect of my daily life. It affected my relationships with family and friends, and for several months, it kept me away from school, sports, and socializing. As painful and lonely as that period in my life was, it also had its silver lining. I learned invaluable coping skills that have served me well ever since.

Coping With Depression at Home

Depression affects your whole family, whether you like it or not. Some family members, such as my mom, seem to naturally know how to help. Others may be less comfortable around you when you're ill. It's not that they don't care. It's just that they aren't sure what to say, so often they don't say anything at all.

While you're wrapped up in your own misery, you may not see what the rest of your family is going through. For instance, it wasn't until later that I realized how hard my depression was on my brother. When I suddenly disappeared from school and then just as suddenly reappeared again, he fielded more questions than I did. He was both bothered and confused by the things he overheard other people saying about me.

By reaching out to your family, you're not only helping yourself. You're supporting them, too. But don't be surprised if it feels forced and uncomfortable at first. Depression tends to make you want to withdraw into a shell, shutting out everyone else. In addition, you might often feel too tired to talk and have trouble staying focused on a conversation for long. Such obstacles come with the territory when you have depression. If you can push past them, however, you may find as I did that communicating with family members gets easier with time.

Talking to Your Parents

Your parents are important allies in your fight against depression. Some parents are more clued in to depression than others, but most sincerely want to help. If you're lucky enough to have a close relationship, your parents can be a source of boundless love and moral support. Because they're older and more experienced, your parents may offer useful advice as well. In addition, you may need your parents' help with practical matters, such as finding a doctor and dealing with insurance. These tips can help you open a dialogue about depression with your parents:

Some parents are more clued in to depression than others, but most sincerely want to help.

- Pick your time carefully. Unless it's an emergency, don't start a discussion just as your parents are rushing off to go to work or drive the carpool. Aim for a time when they'll be more relaxed and attentive.
- Signal that it's important. Tell your parents that you have something serious you want to discuss. If your parents *always* seem to be rushing out the door, ask if they can set aside an hour or so later to talk.
- Plan ahead for what you will say. Try to spell out as clearly as possible what the problem is, how long you've been feeling this way, why you think it's serious, and how you want them to help.
- Write down the key points. That way, you won't forget what you want to say when you and your parents sit down to talk.
- Share this book with them. You might want to mark any sections that seem particularly relevant to your situation.

Helping Yourself to Well-Being

Your parents are invaluable partners in your recovery plan. So are the doctors, therapists, teachers, and other professionals who are working with you and your family. Ultimately, though, the person with the biggest stake in your recovery is *you*. There are many things you can do to foster your own sense of well-being. As you start to improve, these same steps can help reawaken your joy in life:

- Express yourself creatively. For me, art has always been a source of comfort and fulfillment. Even when I hit rock bottom and wound up in the hospital, my sketch pads were a critical outlet for my feelings. You might get the same sense of satisfaction from writing, music, photography, woodworking, cooking, sewing, gardening, or caring for pets. Taking part in a productive hobby is a hopeful, positive act that serves as a powerful antidote to depression.

- Learn to relax and unwind. Often, stress seems to trigger or worsen an episode of depression. It's also harder to concentrate on following your treatment plan and taking care of yourself when you're feeling overwhelmed by stress. In my case, the stressful transition to high school may not have caused my depression directly, but it certainly added to the challenges I faced. For me, spending time in nature and going for walks and bike rides were great stress relievers. Other things you could try include practicing meditation, visualizing yourself in a peaceful setting, or taking a yoga class.
- Nurture your physical health. When you have depression, you learn the hard way how closely your mind and body are linked, because the mental and physical symptoms of this disease go hand in hand. You can turn this mind/body connection to your advantage. When you treat your body with respect and care, you may find that you feel better not only physically, but also emotionally. Energize your body with high-quality fuel, including fruits, vegetables, and whole grains. Get some form of exercise every day. And avoid "quick fixes" that don't really fix anything, such as junk food, alcohol, illegal drugs, and cigarettes.

When you treat your body with respect and care, you may find that you feel better not only physically, but also emotionally.

- Keep tabs on your progress. Once you've identified things that boost your well-being, develop a formal plan for including them in your life on a daily basis. You might also

> **"Alcohol helps me forget how low I'm feeling. Why shouldn't I drink when I'm depressed?"**
>
> It's not uncommon for people with depression to try drowning their pain in alcohol or other drugs. Unfortunately, there's a fundamental flaw in this plan: It doesn't work. While you might feel better temporarily, the good feelings won't last. In the long run, alcohol or drug abuse can make depression worse, and vice versa. Plus, addiction creates a whole new set of problems to worry about. It's no accident that 40% to 60% of those who die by suicide are intoxicated at the time of their deaths.
>
> If you're being treated for depression but still abusing alcohol or drugs, the treatment has less chance of working. You're unlikely to get much out of psychotherapy when you're under the influence. In addition, when you mix alcohol or illegal drugs with prescription medication, they may interact in dangerous ways. On the other hand, when both your depression and your substance abuse are treated at the same time, the odds of a full and lasting recovery are greatly improved.

want to start a journal in which you record what you did and how you felt each day. Now and then, read back through your journal. You'll probably notice some patterns that help you fine-tune your self-care plan. For example, you might notice that your mood is always brighter right after exercise. This may give you the extra incentive to join a sports team or exercise class.

Coping With Depression at School

School was a huge hurdle for me, as it is for many students with depression. If you're a full-time student, you spend more time at school than anywhere else but home. School is the place not only where you learn, but also where you connect with friends and get involved in after-school activities. When you have trouble coping there, the effects can ripple throughout your whole life.

Unfortunately, it's very difficult to do your best academically when your brain is clouded with depression. You may find that it's much harder than usual to pay attention, think clearly, solve problems, and recall information. You also may lose your motivation to study and do homework. Suddenly, making good grades and getting into your dream college may seem like hopeless causes or pointless wastes of time. If you've always thought school was important, and suddenly it seems stupid and trivial, that's a classic example of depression at work.

If you've always thought school was important, and suddenly it seems stupid and trivial, that's a classic example of depression at work.

Working With Your Teachers

Not everyone is as lucky as I was. I attended a small school where most of the teachers knew my family and were eager to help, and I also had the benefit of my own personal teacher at home for a few months. But whatever your situation, there are steps you can take to reduce the academic fallout:

- Enlist the support of teachers. Believe it or not, they're on your side. They want to see you succeed as much as you do, but they can't help if you don't communicate about your needs. Ask your parents to request a conference where you, your parents, and your teachers can all sit down and share information. That may sound like the last thing most students would want to do, but in your situation, it can work to your benefit. For one thing, teachers are less likely to view you as a "discipline problem" when they understand that some changes in your behavior are the symptoms of a mental illness. For another thing, this type of meeting is the first step toward accessing additional help from the school.

- Find creative ways to work around depression. Often, little changes can make a big difference. One of my biggest barriers at school was just making it to class through the crowded hallways. Simply waiting a few minutes until the halls had cleared out helped immensely. Let's say you think this strategy might help you, too. To avoid being counted tardy every day, it just makes sense to talk to your teachers first, explain how this strategy will help you succeed, and ask for their support. Of course, the specific adjustments you request will depend on your situation. If you're having trouble getting things done while you adapt to a new medication, you might ask for extra time on an assignment. If you feel sluggish in the morning, you might try to schedule your most demanding classes later in the day.
- Explore other options, if necessary. For most students with depression, relatively simple changes made through informal channels will probably be enough. However, if your symptoms are especially severe, you might need more extensive help. The Individuals with Disabilities Education Improvement Act of 2004 (IDEA) is the U.S. special education law, which applies to students who have a disability that affects their ability to benefit from general educational services. Some students with mental illness meet the criteria set out by the law. If you think you might need additional services at school, your parent can make a written request for an initial evaluation to determine whether you qualify under IDEA. If you're eligible, you'll receive an individualized educational plan, a written educational plan that outlines the special services you need.

Spending Time With Friends

Even if you're blessed with helpful, caring parents and teachers, they can never take the place of friends your own age. When you're down, you need encouragement and support from your friends more than ever. Looking back, one of the sneakiest ways in which depression undermined my well-being was by making me want to pull back from my friends right when I needed them most.

As you've probably noticed already, all "friends" are not created equal, and a stressful situation such as depression has a way of sorting the best from the rest. Take a long, hard look at your friends, and decide which ones are true supporters for you, the way Liz was for me. Good supporters like to share fun times with you, but they're also there for you when the fun stops. They're willing to listen when you need to talk, and they don't judge, criticize, or make fun of you for having depression. They encourage you to take positive action, but they understand that getting better requires time, and they don't hold you up to unrealistic expectations.

Take a long, hard look at your friends, and decide which ones are true supporters for you.

Meeting all these criteria is a tall order, and it's more than some people will be able to manage. Don't take it personally. Chances are, they're being the best friends they know how to be. If someone close to you isn't acting very supportive, wait for a private moment when you're both feeling calm and relaxed. Then make some gentle but specific suggestions for how they could be more helpful. If this doesn't work, however, you might need to spend less time with that person. When you're already down, you don't need to be around someone who just pulls you lower.

Guy's-Eye View

The sexual feelings that come with adolescence are exciting, but like anything else new, they can be a little awkward or confusing at first. For some teenagers with depression, the confusion may be compounded. Loss of sexual interest is a common symptom of untreated depression. In addition, problems with sexual functioning can be a side effect of treatment with antidepressants, particularly SSRIs. These problems may include lack of sexual desire in both sexes and problems achieving or maintaining an erection in males.

"My sex drive became nonexistent," says Aaron, who developed depression at age 18. "As a result, I questioned my manhood a lot, which put another vicious twist on the depressed thoughts I was already having." Feeling so uncertain about himself, he says, "my sense of self-worth was far too low to think about going out on a date." Aaron's lack of sexual interest didn't improve with the first few antidepressants he tried, but finally he and his doctor found a medication that both decreased his depression symptoms and allowed his normal sexual feelings to come back.

Along with taking this new medication, Aaron made a point of looking for activities that increased his sense of self-esteem and well-being. Aaron says, "I bought an MP3 player with headphones, copied my favorite music onto it, and went walking. I made sure I walked part of the way along the river or through parks, because I enjoyed being surrounded by the beauty of nature." Gradually, he began feeling better about himself, which in turn helped him feel more self-confident about dating. Says Aaron, "I think it's a cause-and-effect thing. When you're feeling healthier on the inside, you're more attractive to other people."

Not everyone with depression experiences sexual problems. But when you have a concern, don't be afraid to bring it up to your doctor. If you're embarrassed, remember that your doctor has heard it before. This is a common problem, and your doctor can help you find the best solution for you.

On the other hand, you should probably make a conscious effort to spend more time with your most supportive friends, even when you don't particularly feel in the mood. Keep it low key. If you're not up to a big night out, just invite a friend or two over to watch a movie or go for a short bike ride in the afternoon. Once you're feeling more energetic, plan fun and interesting activities that you and your friends can enjoy together. Don't forget to take your turn as supporter, too. Unless you're quite severely depressed, aim to give your friends as much attention and encouragement as they give you.

If you don't have anyone like this in your life already, that doesn't mean there's something wrong with you. Many perfectly wonderful people are in the same boat—and they're all looking to make friends, the same way you are. Depression may make it hard for you to believe that anyone would want to be friends with you. When you find yourself thinking this way, remember that it's just the depression telling you lies again. In

To Tell or Not to Tell

Should you tell your friends about your depression? As you've probably gathered by now, I'm a big believer in openness. Your truest friends will accept you, depression and all. And they'll have a better grasp of what's going on when you have a bad spell. Otherwise, they may be mystified or hurt by your behavior. Keep in mind that many people have only vague—and often misinformed—ideas about the causes and nature of depression. By sharing what you've learned, you'll not only educate your friends, but also help them be better, more compassionate supporters.

You'll probably gauge how much to share by the closeness of your relationship. The better you get to know and trust someone, the more comfortable you'll feel talking to that friend about personal thoughts and feelings. If there are certain confidences you want kept private, be sure to say so. Of course, it's important to respect the other person's privacy in turn. (Suicidal remarks are the exception. You should never keep, or expect a friend to keep, such remarks a secret.) Also, remember that depression doesn't have to be your only topic of conversation. Make a point of asking about the other person's life and talking about mutual interests or hobbies.

fact, meeting interesting new people isn't as difficult as you might think:

- Ask a question of the student sitting next to you in class.
- Join a youth group at your school, community center, or church.
- Volunteer for a social, political, or environmental cause you believe in.
- Attend a support group for teenagers with depression.

When you meet someone you like, start a conversation and maybe invite the person to get together casually for an hour or two. Gradually expand your social circle this way. Before long, you'll have a strong network of friends who can help you get through the bad times and inspire fresh hope for better days.

Chapter Seven

One Day at a Time: Recovering from Depression

My Story

My recovery from depression wasn't instantaneous, and it wasn't a nice, steady incline, either. Instead, it was more like a graph with lots of peaks and valleys, but an overall trend that was heading upward. By my sophomore year in high school, I felt well enough to function as a student and do the things a person my age was supposed to be doing. But it wasn't until my junior year that I felt fully recovered.

No one would ever wish to have depression, but I did gain some positive insights from my struggle. It may sound like a cliché, but I hadn't realized what I had until I nearly lost it. Now it was as if someone had hit the reset button on my life. I was back at square one again, and this time, I couldn't wait to get started.

During my junior year, I joined the cross-country track team just for the experience, even though running had never been a talent of mine. I also took part in school plays, traveled to the West Indies as a volunteer, and created some of my most profound artwork. Around town, I was known for the restored car that my dad and I had finally finished. My one-of-a-kind style had morphed into a sense of independence, individuality, and, most of all, confidence.

I was socializing again, but I also remained introspective. I spent much of my out-of-school time alone working on art projects. In school, focusing had become a bit more difficult because of all the thoughts and ideas flooding my mind. As far as my moods went, some days were harder than others. When I became stressed out by day-to-day events, I would start feeling down and discouraged. To combat these feelings, I had a mantra: Take it one day at a time. I reminded myself that a single bad day was just a glitch, not a complete reversal of all my progress.

I reminded myself that a single bad day was just a glitch, not a complete reversal of all my progress.

Finding My Way Home

The summer before my senior year, I heard about a workshop being held at a college in the north woods of Wisconsin. The workshop was designed to introduce high school students to professionals who worked in various environmental fields. It sounded perfect to me. I would be able to camp in the deep woods, learn about Native American lore, meet botanists, go wolf tracking, tag songbirds, and observe loons and bears.

Before this workshop, I wasn't sure whether I wanted to go to college. My art business was thriving. I already had mural jobs lined up for the next year, and if I stayed where I was, it looked as if my reputation as an artist might grow rapidly. But the love of nature was another big part of my total self that I felt shouldn't be neglected. I applied to the workshop, which had limited space, and was thrilled to be accepted. Around midsummer, I headed to the north woods.

I was nervous about being away from familiar surroundings. I had all the standard feelings that come with going somewhere alone for the first time. On top of that, I had added concerns about my mental health and overall stability. I was honest with my mom about those concerns on the car ride to the workshop, but she reminded me of how far I had come and how much strength I had gained.

Within the first five minutes of the workshop, I knew I had made the right choice. I was so swept up in the experience that I didn't have time to worry about whether or not I would be strong enough to handle it. I felt comfortable in these new physical surroundings, but it was more than that. I found that I was not only accepted by my peers there; I was actually celebrated. For the first time, I felt that most of the people around me saw being a bit weird as a desirable quality.

Even after returning home from the workshop, I felt inspired by my experiences there. Now I knew there was a place for me after all, and I decided that this was where I wanted to go for college.

During my senior year, I continued to enjoy myself and embrace my life. But now that I had seen a small glimpse of what was waiting beyond high school, I had the itch to move on to other things. I sensed that my life was going to take the road less traveled, but I didn't want it any other way. To their credit, my family always supported me in my aspirations. They believed that I would be able to make it on my own as a professional artist. They saw that I wasn't afraid to take risks, and I knew they would be there to support me if one of those risks didn't pay off.

Taming the Beast

Halfway through my senior year, I completed the journal about my experiences with depression. I had worked on this journal throughout my illness, drawing the images in my mind and personifying depression as a beast. One day when my uncle was visiting, he saw the journal. His good heart told him that publishing the journal as a book could help others, and his business sense told him it could be successful. He took my journal around to a number of publishing companies, but in its unpolished form, it was rejected by all of them.

I wasn't discouraged by this; I had never intended for my journal to be published in the first place. It was simply one way I dealt with depression—a channel for expressing my thoughts and feelings as I struggled with the illness and its aftermath. My uncle still believed passionately in the power of my story, however, so he decided to self-publish my journal as a book and market it himself.

As graduation grew near, I was juggling several commitments. Aside from school, I was beginning to promote the book, and I was swamped with art commissions. I had worked hard to build a reputation locally as an artist-of-all-trades, doing everything from painting murals in private homes and businesses, to dabbling in graphic design, to building sculptures for special events. My confidence grew day by day, and the thoughts of depression became few and fleeting. I felt balanced, with my head in the clouds and my feet planted firmly on the ground.

I felt honored when people told me they had never been able to talk about their depression before, but felt they could share with me.

The summer after graduation, I began doing more book signings and making presentations about depression. Sometimes my mom joined me, giving the audience the benefit of another perspective. I discovered that speaking to all kinds of people came naturally to me. After I finished a presentation, no matter where I was, someone would always approach to tell me his or her own story. I felt honored when people told me they had never been able to talk about their depression before, but felt they could share with me. Over time, though, I heard a lot of stories that were filled with pain, and I began to let it get me down. I learned a critical lesson: I had to manage my own state of mind and be aware of when I needed a break.

Near summer's end, my uncle, my mom, and I attended a large book convention in Chicago, where we had a booth to promote my book. Ours was just one among 2,000 other booths, and I was a bit overwhelmed by the sea of vendors, publishing companies, and food stands. There were times when I felt some of the old dread and panic creeping back, but whenever I noticed such feelings starting, I would leave for a few minutes to catch my breath. I realized that I had become rather good at checking my responses and doing what I needed to do to stay calm.

While at the convention, I met a literary agent who wanted to represent me. She thought a large publishing house might be interested in my book, and I agreed that this sounded fine. To be honest, though, I didn't give it much thought after I got home. I was busy with all the exciting changes in my life and distracted by the pull of other dreams.

Leaving for College

The last weeks of summer were spent with Liz and a few other close friends. We would be heading off in different directions soon, and we were all a little nervous about starting our brand-new adult lives. I had an extra dimension to my anxiety, though, and my brain felt like it was erupting with questions and concerns: Would I be able to adjust to my new environment at college? Would my medicine keep working? Would I be able to handle daily life on my own?

Just as I had planned, I was enrolling at the Wisconsin college where I had attended the workshop. This small liberal arts and environmental college was about ten hours away from home, so I knew I wouldn't be seeing my family very often. It felt as if I was going to be a million miles away.

Yet it only took a few hours after arriving at college to feel as if I had been there for years. I felt a certain freedom in being someplace where no one had any preconceived ideas about me or my background. I knew that the chance for a fresh start doesn't come along very often, and I was determined to take full advantage of it. I felt as if I had my whole life right in front of me.

Within a couple of weeks, however, I was already facing a problem. After being on medication for a few years, I had come to take its necessity for granted. I really didn't think about it much anymore. I just took my meds, and my moods felt even. Unfortunately, I had trouble getting my medication at the pharmacy in the college town, so I went without it for a little over a week. For the first couple of days, I was doing all right, but I felt like a ticking bomb. I was worried about a looming collapse.

It came during a kayaking class. There I was in Lake Superior on a beautiful fall day in the company of my new friends. We were paddling along the shoreline into the sunset, when out of nowhere I began to cry. Sadness felt like it was clawing its way up my throat, struggling to release itself. I knew that what I was feeling was only due to the absence of my medication, and I also knew that I would be getting my meds again in a couple of days. But that knowledge didn't subdue the sadness, so I lagged behind the rest of my class and tried to collect myself.

In the end, I wound up acknowledging my depression to a whole new group of classmates. To my surprise, no one thought any less of me. In fact, I gained the respect accorded to anyone who has overcome great odds. My friends' acceptance just confirmed that I had found the right place for me.

Back home, my mom said the house was a lot quieter once I was gone. She missed having me around to talk to. She missed seeing the projects I was involved in. She even said she missed the little messes I would leave around the house. I think the pain was amplified for her because of how close we had grown during my illness. We had been through a lot together, and it was an adjustment for both of us getting along without that daily interaction and support. Ultimately, though, I know my mom was proud to see how independent I had become.

As time went on, things back home changed even more. My parents got a divorce, and the first couple of years afterward were extremely difficult for my whole family. Yet in the long run, the divorce may have been the best thing for my dad, because it brought up issues that forced him to confront his own depression. After a past of many half-hearted attempts at treatment, he finally stuck with counseling and stayed on his medication. Eventually, my dad began giving lectures about men and depression. His speeches, which drew on his personal experiences and were filled with honest sharing, never failed to move an audience.

Midway through my freshman year at college, I received a phone call from the literary agent I had met the previous summer in Chicago. She informed me that four major publishing companies were bidding on the rights to my book. My initial reaction was to think that someone must be playing a joke, but soon it dawned on me that this call was for real. I was stunned—they actually wanted my book! I felt like I was still in shock for hours after I hung up the phone.

Eventually, a big publishing company did buy the rights to my book, and over the next few months, I worked on fine-tuning the illustrations and text. The book was released during my sophomore year at college. I toured off and on that year to promote it, and I also did media interviews over the phone. It was a challenge balancing my new role as an author with my responsibilities as a student. But it was also a gift—a way to salvage something positive and meaningful from the wreckage of my suffering.

My Life, Today and Tomorrow

Today I'm 26, and it has been 12 years since I first found myself in the grips of the beast. The book you're holding in your hands is my second foray into being an author, and my art business is thriving as well. Depression is still an unwanted stowaway in my mind, and I know it probably always will be. But I work at managing my illness on a daily basis, and although it isn't always easy, I usually keep the beast at bay.

As I've grown older, my concerns have naturally evolved, too: Will I always be able to afford my medication? Can I get an appointment with my doctor? I also wonder about my future relationships: What will marriage be like? Will I find someone who wants to stay with me even if the beast resurfaces from time to time? And I worry about what fresh tricks the beast might have in store: Will my medicine keep working? How long will I be able to maintain my emotional balance?

The difference is that now I know a downturn isn't the end of the story. I've learned to trust that happier chapters lie ahead, and I've gained strength from knowing how much I can endure and still survive.

Use your strength to pull the pain out of yourself and into the world, where you can confront it.

I hope my story will inspire you to find that last bit of strength within yourself, too. At times, it may be nearly obscured by the darkness, but it's still there. Use your strength to pull the pain out of yourself and into the world, where you can confront it. This takes tremendous courage, but the rewards you'll reap are even greater. Once you start feeling better, hold tight to the knowledge of your progress, and never forget the strength and courage that brought you there.

Some Frequently Asked Questions

Understanding Depression

My aunt says not to worry; all teenagers have mood swings. Isn't depression just a normal part of being my age?

A depressed mood that causes you deep distress or seriously interferes with your life isn't normal at any age. It's every bit as painful and disruptive at 18 as it is at 28, 38, or 98, and the consequences of leaving depression untreated can be just as severe as well. Fortunately, depression can be diagnosed and treated in teenagers and young adults the same as it is in older people. So if you're struggling, don't assume it's just "moodiness." Consult a mental health professional, who can help you determine whether what you're feeling is actually due to a treatable disorder.

I've already been diagnosed with depression. Does that mean I'll have it for the rest of my life?

Research is currently under way to find better treatments and eventually a cure for depression. For now, however, there isn't a cure. Once you've had an episode of depression, you're at increased risk for future episodes. In fact, three out of five people who have had one bout of major depression go on to have another. So it's probably best to think of this as a disease you'll carry with you for life. You'll need to keep monitoring your moods and paying attention to your lifestyle indefinitely, and you might need to remain in treatment long-term as well.

That doesn't mean you'll be suffering forever, though. With treatment, there's an excellent chance you'll start to feel better and be able to get on with your life. But because a relapse or recurrence is always a possibility, you should be on the lookout for early warning signs. You also need to be extra conscientious about taking care of your health, by getting enough relaxation and sleep, exercising regularly, eating healthfully, and building a strong social support network. And if your doctor recommends maintenance therapy—in other words, long-term treatment aimed at preventing a recurrence—you would do well to heed the advice.

Getting the Treatment You Need

What factors should my parents and I consider when choosing my mental health treatment provider?

These are some questions you or your parents might want to ask when looking for a psychiatrist or therapist.

Questions for the office staff before your first visit

- What kind of licensure and credentials does the provider have?
- Where is the office located?
- What are the office hours?
- Does the provider accept your insurance plan?

- Is there a sliding scale for fees that aren't covered by insurance?
- How long will you have to wait for your first appointment?

Questions for the provider at the first visit

- Do you consider yourself a specialist in mood disorders?
- How many of your patients are adolescents?
- What is your general philosophy about the role of medications?
- Can you prescribe medication? If not, are you willing to coordinate care with a prescribing doctor if necessary?
- What is your general philosophy about the role of psychotherapy?
- Do you provide therapy? If not, are you willing to coordinate care with a therapist if that turns out to be appropriate?

How can I tell if I've actually found the right therapist for me?

Psychotherapy is a collaborative process. Within the first few sessions, you should begin getting a feel for how that process is going. Ideally, you should have a sense of rapport with your therapist. That doesn't mean you and your therapist will become friends in the usual sense, and it also doesn't mean that therapy will be fun and games. But it does mean you should feel safe opening up about your thoughts and feelings in an atmosphere of trust and mutual respect.

Therapy is hard work, and at times your therapist may push you to do things you don't particularly want to do. That's part of the process. However, you should be able to trust that your therapist is acting in your best interests, and you should have confidence that your therapist knows what he or she is doing. If either of these elements is missing, talk to your therapist about your concerns. In most cases, you'll probably be able to resolve the issue. But if your concerns aren't addressed satisfactorily or taken seriously, it might be time to look for a new therapist.

How long should I wait before concluding that a particular medication isn't working for me?

The best person to answer that question is the doctor who prescribed the medication. Keep in mind, though, that it may take four to six weeks to feel the full effects of an antidepressant, so you might need to be patient. If you don't stick with your medication long enough to give it a fair trial, you're only shortchanging yourself. After the designated period has passed, if you still aren't feeling better, talk to your doctor about your options. Don't just stop the medication on your own, however, because that could cause your symptoms to get worse.

I don't like taking medicine. Can't I treat my depression with herbs, acupuncture, or some other alternative therapy?

By definition, alternative therapies haven't been subjected to the same rigorous testing as conventional medical treatments. Therefore, they haven't been shown to be safe and effective in scientific studies. If they had, they would become standard treatments, and they wouldn't be considered "alternative" anymore.

Some therapies that are currently unproven might eventually turn out to be helpful for depression, but others might have no effect, and still others might actually be harmful. It doesn't make sense to gamble with your health by using an unproven treatment *in place of* a proven one, such as medication or psychotherapy. If you're interested in trying an alternative therapy *in addition to* your other treatment, it's still wise to talk to your doctor or therapist first to make sure the treatments are compatible. For example, some herbs are known to interact harmfully with certain medications.

Battling Stereotypes and Stigma

Does having depression really mean I'm mentally ill?

Depression is considered a mental illness, but that's not as scary as it might sound. A mental illness is a brain disorder that affects your thoughts, moods, emotions, or complex behaviors, such as interacting with other people or planning future activities.

Unfortunately, there are a lot of misconceptions about mental illness. Some people mistakenly believe that everyone with a mental illness loses touch with reality, behaves bizarrely, or acts violently or self-destructively. Because the term "mental illness" has become so emotionally charged, you might feel more comfortable referring to depression as a "brain disorder." That's totally up to you, however. In theory, there should be no difference between saying you have a mental illness and saying you have diabetes, heart disease, or asthma.

Okay, I get it, but not everyone does. How can I respond when people make hurtful or uninformed remarks?

Some people think depression is "all in your mind" or believe you can "just snap out of it." You'll be doing them a favor if you politely set the record straight. Give them the benefit of the doubt. Unless you know otherwise, assume that they're speaking out of ignorance rather than maliciousness. Explain that depression is a real illness that's not just in your mind, but also in your brain and the rest of your body. Although you can't snap out of it, you can get treatment. But even the best treatment takes time to work. Let people know you're getting better as fast as you can, and you'll appreciate their patience and understanding in the meantime.

As already noted, you may also run into some people who believe that having a mental illness means you're "crazy" and unable to fit into society. Once again, the best antidote to negative stereotypes is a healthy dose of the truth. Fortunately, the stigma attached to mental illness seems to have been lessening in recent decades. You might find that people your own age are more comfortable with the idea of a mental illness than those your parents' or grandparents' age.

What else can I do to get the word out about depression?

If you're interested in tackling stigma on a broader scale, consider volunteering for one of the organizations listed in the Resources section of this book. Several have active advocacy programs, which strive to influence public policy at the local, state, and federal level through a variety of activities. Among the groups advocating on behalf of people with depression are the Depression and Bipolar Support Alliance (www.dbsalliance.org), National Alliance on Mental Illness (NAMI, www.nami.org), National Mental Health Association (www.nmha.org), Child and Adolescent Bipolar Foundation (www.cabf.org), Suicide Prevention Action Network USA (SPAN USA, www.spanusa.org), and American Foundation for Suicide Prevention (www.afsp.org).

Among the key issues that advocates address are making mental health services more available and affordable as well as protecting the rights of people with mental illness at school and work. Advocates might champion their cause by lobbying legislators or launching a media campaign to educate the public. If that appeals to you, consider volunteering your time and talents. You could also get involved by writing to your legislators, talking to the media, giving presentations at school, or participating in fundraisers. And of course, as soon as you're 18, voting in every election is another way to make your voice heard.

Entering the Adult World

I'll be leaving for college soon. Should I be worried about how I'll adjust?

As a college student with depression, you'll be far from alone. A recent survey by the American College Health Association, which included more than 54,000 students at 71 colleges, found that 16% said they had been formally diagnosed with depression at some point. Many more said they struggled with depression-like thoughts and feelings from time to time. For example, 46% said they had felt so depressed that it was hard to function at least once in the past year, and 10% said they had seriously considered suicide.

Alison Malmon is the 24-year-old founder and executive director of Active Minds, a student-run mental health awareness group with more than 40 chapters on college campuses across the country. According to Malmon, "Your freshman year is critical, because big changes in your life can trigger underlying mental health issues. In your second year, you might be hit with a sophomore slump and feel like nobody cares about you anymore, which can also bring out depression. If you go abroad to study, coming back in your junior year is often a really difficult transition, and that sometimes precipitates a mental health crisis as well. Then in your senior year, you're faced with the stress and anxiety of trying to decide what to do with your whole life, and those feelings might contribute to depression, too."

In other words, college is not only an exciting time, but also potentially a stressful one. If you're already predisposed to depression, the stress might sometimes trigger new symptoms or worsen existing ones. Having depression certainly doesn't rule out succeeding at college, though. In any large lecture class, there's a good chance that dozens of students have depression, and many of them are probably doing just fine despite their illness. You, too, can still meet the challenges of college successfully, but it helps to plan ahead for how you'll cope.

So how can I handle the challenges of college effectively?

The best time to start devising your coping plan is while you're still choosing a college. When you're checking out dorm rooms, courses, and nightlife, be sure to ask about student counseling and mental health services, too. Student counseling centers often provide excellent guidance on typical college issues, such as roommate conflicts, academic pressure, and mild sadness or anxiety. However, counseling centers generally don't offer long-term care or treatment for more severe problems, such as major depression. For that, you'll need to see a treatment provider at the campus medical center or in the surrounding community.

Here are some questions you may want to ask:

- What mental health services are provided on campus for free?
- What campus services will you need to pay for? How much are the fees, and will your insurance cover them?
- Will you need to go off-campus for some services? If so, it's smart to find a treatment provider before you leave for college. Does the provider offer discounted fees for students? Is it easy to get to the provider's office?

- Does the campus medical center have a pharmacy? If so, will it fill prescriptions from outside providers? Does it carry your medication?
- Where can you turn if you're having a serious crisis? Ask what numbers to call in case of emergency—days, evenings, and weekends.

It's also important to establish a new support network of friends and classmates as soon as possible. If you'll be moving away from home, living in a dorm can be a great way to make friends quickly. Other good ways to meet like-minded people include joining student clubs, taking part in study groups, and getting involved in campus activities. Sports, theater, the student newspaper, environmental or political causes—most colleges cater to a wide range of student interests and hobbies. In addition, many host mental health support and advocacy groups. Two of the larger ones are Active Minds (www.activemindsoncampus.org) and NAMI on Campus (www.nami.org), but ask what's available at your school.

I'll be living on my own for the first time soon. How can I keep my recovery on track?

Whether you plan to go to college or work, moving out of your parents' house for the first time is always a major milestone. The more preparation you can do, the better. About a year before you'll be moving out, gradually start taking over more responsibility for yourself. That can mean everything from doing laundry and cooking meals, to budgeting money and paying bills, to making your own doctor and therapist appointments and driving yourself to them.

Once you're on your own, lavish yourself with the same attention and nurturing that your parents gave you—or that you wish they'd given you, if your home life wasn't all it could have been. Plan your days carefully, leaving enough time for exercise and sleep as well as study or work. Set up a system for remembering to take your medication; for example, by using a weekly pillbox with a compartment for each day and keeping it in a prominent place. Continue seeing your doctor and/or therapist, or find new ones in your new community. And don't forget to make time for fun—hanging out with friends and doing things you enjoy are therapeutic.

Will I eventually have a career, a family, and all the things I've dreamed of?

There aren't any guarantees in life, depression or not. However, there's no reason your illness has to hold you back. Yes, depression is a hurdle to overcome, but there are treatments and resources available to help. As you tackle this hurdle, you may find that you're stronger and more capable than you ever imagined. That's a priceless self-discovery you might not have made otherwise. The pride and self-confidence you gain as a result will serve you well in whatever you do for the rest of your life.

Glossary

advocacy Efforts to influence public policy at the local, state, and federal level through a variety of activities.

antidepressant A medication used to prevent or relieve depression.

anxiety disorder A disorder characterized by excessive fear or worry that either lasts a long time or recurs again and again.

attention-deficit hyperactivity disorder (ADHD) A disorder characterized by a short attention span, excessive activity, or impulsive behavior.

bipolar disorder A disorder characterized by an overly high mood, called mania, that alternates with depression.

chronic disease A disease that lasts a long time or recurs frequently over an extended period.

cognitive-behavioral therapy A form of psychotherapy that aims to change habitual patterns of thinking and behavior that may be contributing to a person's problems.

comorbidity The presence of two or more disorders at once in the same person.

computed tomography (CT) scan An imaging test that uses special x-ray equipment and a powerful computer to create cross-sectional images of tissues and organs inside the body.

conduct disorder A disorder characterized by a pattern of extreme difficulty following rules or conforming to social norms.

crisis residential treatment Temporary, 24-hour mental health care in a nonhospital setting during a crisis.

depression A feeling of being sad, hopeless, or apathetic that lasts for at least a couple of weeks. See major depression.

dysthymia A disorder that involves being either depressed or irritable most of the day. The symptoms are relatively mild, but long-lasting. They occur more days than not for at least a year.

eating disorder A disorder characterized by serious disturbances in eating behavior. People may severely restrict what they eat, or they may go on eating binges, then try to compensate by means such as self-induced vomiting or misuse of laxatives.

electroconvulsive therapy (ECT) A treatment for depression that involves delivering a carefully controlled electrical current to the brain, where it produces a brief seizure. This is thought to alter some of the electrical and chemical processes involved in brain functioning.

employee assistance program (EAP) A confidential information, support, and referral service that many employers provide for employees and their family members who are having problems with daily living or emotional well-being.

explanatory style The way people habitually explain to themselves why events happen.

family therapy Psychotherapy that brings together several members of a family for therapy sessions.

group therapy Psychotherapy that brings together several patients with similar diagnoses or issues for therapy sessions.

hospitalization Inpatient treatment in a facility that provides intensive, specialized care and close, round-the-clock monitoring.

hypersomnia Excessive sleepiness, as shown by sleeping too long at night or having trouble staying alert and awake during the day.

individualized educational plan A written educational plan for a student who qualifies for services under the Individuals with Disabilities Education Improvement Act of 2004.

Individuals with Disabilities Education Improvement Act of 2004 (IDEA) The U.S. special education law, which applies to students who have a disability that affects their ability to benefit from general educational services.

insomnia Trouble falling or staying asleep, or getting sleep of such poor quality that the person doesn't feel rested and refreshed the next morning.

learning disorder A disorder that adversely affects a person's performance in school or ability to function in everyday situations that call for reading, writing, or math.

light therapy A therapeutic regimen of daily exposure to very bright light from an artificial source.

maintenance therapy Long-term treatment aimed at preventing a recurrence.

major depression A disorder that involves being either depressed or irritable nearly all the time, or losing interest or enjoyment in almost everything. These feelings last for at least two weeks. They are associated with several other symptoms, and they cause significant distress or difficulty with everyday activities.

mania An overly high mood that lasts for at least a week or leads to dangerous behavior. Symptoms include overblown ideas, racing thoughts, risk taking, extreme irritability, decreased need for sleep, and increased talkativeness or activity.

manic depression See bipolar disorder.

Medicaid A government program that provides medical and mental health care to those who meet eligibility criteria.

melatonin A hormone that regulates the body's internal clock, which controls the timing of daily fluctuations in sleep, body temperature, and hormone secretion.

mental illness A brain disorder that affects thoughts, moods, emotions, or complex behaviors, such as interacting with other people or planning future activities.

minor depression A term sometimes used to describe a situation in which a person has some symptoms of depression, but these symptoms are fewer and less severe than those seen in major depression.

monoamine oxidase inhibitor (MAOI) An older class of antidepressant that is rarely prescribed for young people.

mood A pervasive emotion that colors a person's whole view of the world.

neurotransmitter A chemical that acts as a messenger within the brain.

norepinephrine A neurotransmitter that plays a role in the body's response to stress and helps regulate arousal, sleep, and blood pressure.

outpatient treatment A treatment option where you live at home and go to school as usual, but occasionally see a doctor or therapist.

partial hospitalization A treatment option where you spend at least four hours a day on therapy and other treatment-related services, but go home at night.

pessimistic thinking style A tendency to believe that bad events are unchangeable, will undermine everything a person does, and are that person's own fault, regardless of evidence to the contrary.

placebo A sugar pill that looks like a real medication but doesn't contain any active ingredient.

premenstrual dysphoric disorder (PMDD) A cyclic disorder in which a woman has severe, disabling emotional and physical symptoms right before her menstrual period. These symptoms begin to subside within a few days after her period starts, and they disappear in the week after her period ends.

psychiatrist A medical doctor who specializes in the diagnosis and treatment of mental illnesses and emotional problems.

psychologist A mental health professional who provides assessment and treatment for mental and emotional disorders.

psychotherapy The treatment of a mental disorder with "talk therapy" and other psychological techniques.

receptor A molecule that recognizes a specific chemical, such as a neurotransmitter. For a chemical message to be sent from one nerve cell to another, it must be delivered to a matching receptor on the receiving cell.

recurrence A repeat episode of an illness after a lengthy period of feeling back to normal.

relapse The reappearance of symptoms after going away for a short time.

residential treatment center A treatment facility where you live in a dorm-like setting with a group of people your age. The treatment there is less specialized and intensive than in a hospital, but the length of stay is often much longer.

reuptake The process by which a neurotransmitter is absorbed back into the cell that originally released it.

seasonal affective disorder (SAD) A form of depression in which the symptoms come and go around the same time each year. Typically, the symptoms begin in the fall or winter and subside in the spring.

selective serotonin reuptake inhibitor (SSRI) An widely prescribed type of antidepressant. SSRIs work by interfering with the absorption of serotonin back into the brain cells that first released it.

serotonin A neurotransmitter that plays a role in mood and helps regulate sleep, appetite, and sexual drive.

side effect An unintended effect of a medication.

St. John's wort *(Hypericum perforatum)* An herb that is a popular dietary supplement.

State Child Health Insurance Program (SCHIP) A government program that provides free or low-cost insurance coverage for children and teenagers whose families meet eligibility criteria.

stress response The body's response to any perceived threat—real or imagined, physical or psychological. It sets off physiological changes, such as an increase in heart rate, blood pressure, breathing rate, and muscle tension.

support group A group of people with a common problem who get together to share emotional support and practical advice.

synapse The gap between two nerve cells.

transporter A large molecule that is involved in bringing a neurotransmitter back to the cell that originally sent it out.

tricyclic antidepressant An older type of depression medication.

Resources

Organizations

All of these organizations provide information about some aspect of depression, suicide, or mental illness. Those marked with an asterisk (*) also offer a searchable online directory of mental health care providers.

Active Minds on Campus
1875 Connecticut Ave., NW, Suite 418
Washington, DC 20009
(202) 719-1177
www.activemindsoncampus.org

***American Academy of Child and Adolescent Psychiatry**
3615 Wisconsin Ave., NW
Washington, DC 20016
(202) 966-7300
www.aacap.org
www.parentsmedguide.org

American Association of Suicidology
5221 Wisconsin Ave., NW
Washington, DC 20015
(202) 237-2280
www.suicidology.org

American Foundation for Suicide Prevention
120 Wall St., 22nd Floor
New York, NY 10005
(888) 333-2377
www.afsp.org

American Psychiatric Association
1000 Wilson Blvd., Suite 1825
Arlington, VA 22209
(888) 357-7924
www.psych.org
www.healthyminds.org

***American Psychological Association**
750 First St., NE
Washington, DC 20002
(800) 374-2721
www.apa.org
www.apahelpcenter.org

Bazelon Center for Mental Health Law
1101 15th St., NW, Suite 1212
Washington, DC 20005
(202) 467-5730
www.bazelon.org

Child and Adolescent Bipolar Foundation
1000 Skokie Blvd., Suite 570
Wilmette, IL 60091
(847) 256-8525
www.bpKids.org

Depression and Bipolar Support Alliance
730 N. Franklin St., Suite 501
Chicago, IL 60610
(800) 826-3632
www.dbsalliance.org

Depression and Related Affective Disorders Association
8201 Greensboro Dr., Suite 300
McLean, VA 22102
(703) 610-9026
www.drada.org
www.depressedteens.com

Families for Depression Awareness
395 Totten Pond Rd., Suite 404
Waltham, MA 02451
(781) 890-0220
www.familyaware.org

Jed Foundation
583 Broadway, Suite 8B
New York, NY 10012
(212) 647-7544
www.jedfoundation.org

NARSAD, The National Mental Health Research Association
60 Cutter Mill Rd., Suite 404
Great Neck, NY 11021
(800) 829-8289
www.narsad.org

National Alliance on Mental Illness
Colonial Place Three
2107 Wilson Blvd., Suite 300
Arlington, VA 22201
(800) 950-6264
www.nami.org

***National Association of Social Workers**
750 First St., NE, Suite 700
Washington, DC 20002
(202) 408-8600
www.socialworkers.org
www.helpstartshere.org

National Disability Rights Network
900 Second St., NE, Suite 211
Washington, DC 20002
(202) 408-9514
www.napas.org

National Institute of Mental Health
6001 Executive Blvd., Room 8184, MSC 9663
Bethesda, MD 20892
(866) 615-6464
www.nimh.nih.gov

National Mental Health Association
2000 N. Beauregard St., 6th Floor
Alexandria, VA 22311
(800) 969-6642
www.nmha.org

***National Mental Health Information Center**
P.O. Box 42557
Washington, DC 20015
(800) 789-2647
www.mentalhealth.samhsa.gov

Suicide Awareness Voices of Education
9001 E. Bloomington Freeway, Suite 150
Bloomington, MN 55420
(952) 946-7998
www.save.org

Suicide Prevention Action Network USA
1025 Vermont Ave., NW, Suite 1066
Washington, DC 20005
(202) 449-3600
www.spanusa.org

Books

Some of these books are more challenging to read than others, but all are worth the effort. Those written specifically for teens or young adults are marked with a dagger (†).

†Cobain, Bev. *When Nothing Matters Anymore: A Survival Guide for Depressed Teens.* Minneapolis, MN: Free Spirit, 1998.

†Copeland, Mary Ellen, and Stuart Copans. *Recovering From Depression: A Workbook for Teens* (rev. ed.). Baltimore, MD: Paul H. Brookes, 2002.

DePaulo, J. Raymond Jr., and Leslie Alan Horvitz. *Understanding Depression: What We Know and What You Can Do About It.* New York: John Wiley, 2002.

Jamison, Kay Redfield. *Night Falls Fast: Understanding Suicide.* New York: Vintage, 2000.

†Nelson, Richard E., and Judith C. Galas. *The Power to Prevent Suicide: A Guide for Teens Helping Teens.* Minneapolis, MN: Free Spirit, 1994.

Rosenthal, Norman E. *Winter Blues: Everything You Need to Know to Beat Seasonal Affective Disorder* (rev. ed.). New York: Guilford, 2006.
Thase, Michael E., and Susan S. Lang. *Beating the Blues: New Approaches to Overcoming Dysthymia and Chronic Mild Depression* (new ed.). New York: Oxford University Press, 2006.

First-Person Accounts

Casey, Nell (Ed.). *Unholy Ghost: Writers on Depression.* New York: Perennial, 2002.
†Irwin, Cait. *Conquering the Beast Within: How I Fought Depression and Won . . . And How You Can, Too.* New York: Three Rivers, 1998.
†Jamieson, Patrick E., with Moira A. Rynn. *Mind Race: A Firsthand Account of One Teenager's Experience With Bipolar Disorder.* New York: Oxford University Press with the Annenberg Foundation Trust at Sunnylands and the Annenberg Public Policy Center at the University of Pennsylvania, 2006.
Manning, Martha. *Undercurrents: A Life Beneath the Surface.* New York: HarperCollins, 1994.
Solomon, Andrew. *The Noonday Demon: An Atlas of Depression.* New York: Scribner, 2001.
Styron, William. *Darkness Visible: A Memoir of Madness.* New York: Vintage, 1992.
Thompson, Tracy. *The Beast: A Journey Through Depression.* New York: Plume, 1996.

Biographical Accounts

Shenk, Joshua Wolf. *Lincoln's Melancholy: How Depression Challenged a President and Fueled His Greatness.* Boston: Houghton Mifflin, 2005.

Hotlines

National Hopeline Network, Kristin Brooks Hope Center, (800) 784-2433, www.hopeline.com
National Suicide Prevention Lifeline, Substance Abuse and Mental Health Services Administration, (800) 273-8255, www.suicidepreventionlifeline.org

Web Sites

MindZone, Annenberg Foundation Trust at Sunnylands with the Annenberg Public Policy Center of the University of Pennsylvania, www.copecaredeal.org
TeensHealth, Nemours Foundation, www.teenshealth.org

Help for Related Problems

Anxiety Disorders

Organizations

Anxiety Disorders Association of America
(240) 485-1001
www.adaa.org

Freedom From Fear
(718) 351-1717
www.freedomfromfear.org

Books

Ford, Emily, with Michael Liebowitz and Linda Wasmer Andrews. *What You Must Think of Me: A Firsthand Account of One Teenager's Experience with Social Anxiety Disorder*. New York: Oxford University Press with the Annenberg Foundation Trust at Sunnylands and the Annenberg Public Policy Center at the University of Pennsylavnia, forthcoming 2007.

Attention-Deficit Hyperactivity Disorder

Organizations

Attention Deficit Disorder Association
(484) 945-2101
www.add.org

Children and Adults with Attention-Deficit/Hyperactivity Disorder
(800) 233-4050
www.chadd.org, www.help4adhd.org

Conduct Disorder

Organizations

National Runaway Switchboard
(800) 786-2929
www.nrscrisisline.org

National Youth Violence Prevention Resource Center
(866) 723-3968
www.safeyouth.org

Eating Disorders

Organizations

Academy for Eating Disorders
(847) 498-4274
www.aedweb.org

National Association of Anorexia Nervosa and Associated Disorders
(847) 831-3438
www.anad.org

National Eating Disorders Association
(800) 931-2237
www.nationaleatingdisorders.org

Book

†Arnold, Carrie, with B. Timothy Walsh. *Next to Nothing: A Firsthand Account of One Teenager's Experience with an Eating Disorder*. New York: Oxford University Press with the Annenberg Foundation Trust at Sunnylands and the Annenberg Public Policy Center at the University of Pennsylvania, forthcoming 2007.

Web Site

Anorexia Nervosa and Related Eating Disorders, www.anred.com

Substance Abuse

Organizations

Alcoholics Anonymous
(212) 870-3400 (check your phone book for a local number)
www.aa.org

American Council for Drug Education
(800) 488-3784
www.acde.org

Narcotics Anonymous
(818) 773-9999
www.na.org

National Council on Alcoholism and Drug Dependence
(800) 622-2255
www.ncadd.org

National Institute on Alcohol Abuse and Alcoholism
(301) 443–3860
www.niaaa.nih.gov, www.collegedrinkingprevention.gov

National Institute on Drug Abuse
(301) 443-1124
www.drugabuse.gov, teens.drugabuse.gov

Partnership for a Drug-Free America
(212) 922-1560
www.drugfreeamerica.com

Substance Abuse and Mental Health Services Administration
(800) 729-6686
ncadi.samhsa.gov, csat.samhsa.gov, prevention.samhsa.gov

Web Sites

Facts on Tap, Phoenix House, www.factsontap.org
Freevibe, National Youth Anti-Drug Media Campaign, www.freevibe.com
The New Science of Addiction: Genetics and the Brain, Genetic Science Learning Center at the University of Utah, learn.genetics.utah.edu/units/addiction

Bibliography

Books

American Psychiatric Association. *Diagnostic and Statistical Manual of Mental Disorders* (4th ed., text revision). Washington, DC: American Psychiatric Association, 2000.

Evans, Dwight L., and Linda Wasmer Andrews. *If Your Adolescent Has Depression or Bipolar Disorder: An Essential Resource for Parents.* New York: Oxford University Press with the Annenberg Foundation Trust at Sunnylands and the Annenberg Public Policy Center at the University of Pennsylvania, 2005.

Evans, Dwight L., Edna B. Foa, Raquel E. Gur, Herbert Hendin, Charles P. O'Brien, Martin E. P. Seligman, and B. Timothy Walsh (eds.). *Treating and Preventing Adolescent Mental Health Disorders: What We Know and What We Don't Know.* New York: Oxford University Press with the Annenberg Foundation Trust at Sunnylands and the Annenberg Public Policy Center of the University of Pennsylvania, 2005.

Reports

American College Health Association. *American College Health Association-National College Health Assessment: Reference Group Executive Summary, Spring 2005.* Baltimore, MD: American College Health Association, 2005.

Grunbaum, Jo Anne, Laura Kann, Steve Kinchen, James Ross, Joseph Hawkins, Richard Lowry et al. *Youth Risk Behavior Surveillance—United States, 2003* (*MMWR Surveillance Summaries* 53, no. SS-2). Atlanta, GA: Centers for Disease Control and Prevention, 2004.

Journal Articles

Hypericum Depression Trial Study Group. Effect of *Hypericum perforatum* (St. John's Wort) in major depressive disorder: A randomized controlled trial. *JAMA* 287 (April 10, 2002): 1807-1814.

Kessler, Ronald C., Patricia Berglund, Olga Demler, Robert Jin, Kathleen R. Merikangas, and Ellen E. Walters. Lifetime prevalence and age-of-onset distributions of *DSM-IV* disorders in the National Comorbidity Survey Replication. *Archives of General Psychiatry* 62 (June 2005): 593-602.

Saluja, Gitanjali, Ronaldo Iachan, Peter C. Scheidt, Mary D. Overpeck, Wenyu Sun, and Jay N. Giedd. Prevalence of and risk factors for depressive symptoms among young adolescents. *Archives of Pediatric and Adolescent Medicine* 158 (August 2004): 760-765.

Treatment for Adolescents With Depression Study (TADS) Team. Fluoxetine, cognitive-behavioral therapy, and their combination for adolescents with depression: Treatment for Adolescents With Depression Study (TADS) randomized controlled trial. *JAMA* 292 (August 18, 2004): 807-820.

Index